ELEMENTS OF WRITING

Elements of Writing

ROBERT SCHOLES
BROWN UNIVERSITY

CARL H. KLAUS
UNIVERSITY OF IOWA

New York
OXFORD UNIVERSITY PRESS
London 1972 Toronto

Passages from works by the following writers were made possible by the kind permission of their respective publishers.

ANTHONY BURGESS   from *A Clockwork Orange.* Copyright © 1962 by Anthony Burgess. Copyright © 1963 by W. W. Norton and Co., Inc. Reprinted by permission of W. W. Norton and Co., Inc., and William Heinemann Ltd.

ELDRIDGE CLEAVER   from *Soul on Ice.* Copyright © 1968 by Eldridge Cleaver. Reprinted by permission of McGraw-Hill Book Co.

CYRIL CONNOLLY   from *The Unquiet Grave.* Reprinted by permission of Harper and Row, Publishers, and Hamish Hamilton, Ltd.

ERNEST HEMINGWAY from *Death in the Afternoon,* pp. 274-75. Copyright 1932 Charles Scribner's Sons; renewal copyright © 1960 Ernest Hemingway. From *In Our Time,* p. 23. Copyright 1925 Charles Scribner's Sons; copyright renewed 1953 Ernest Hemingway. Both selections reprinted by permission of the publisher. The cable from Hemingway is quoted in Charles Fenton, *The Apprenticeship of Ernest Hemingway.* Copyright © 1954 by Charles Fenton. Reprinted by permission of the author and Farrar, Straus and Giroux, Inc.

JAMES JOYCE—from *Ulysses.* Copyright © 1914, 1918, 1942, 1946 by Nora Joseph Joyce. Reprinted by permission of Random House, Inc., and The Bodley Head.

A Note for Those Who May Use This Book

This is a little book about writing. We have kept its size down, not because there isn't a lot to be said about writing, but because reading about writing is one of the least rewarding activities known to civilized man. In the scale of human interest it ranks right around watching a bowling match on television. Of course, books on the art of writing have a redeeming social value that raises them far above the level of bowling. Or they would if they actually helped people to write better. But do they? Most don't. We say that flatly, on the basis of our combined thirty years in the classroom teaching English. The teacher may ease his conscience by requiring his students to buy some grand compendium of compositional advice, but the chances of such a tome's ever helping a student to write better are very small indeed. What is accomplished in the formal study of writing (whether it is called Freshman English, Composition, Rhetoric, or Communications, or hidden behind some grander title) is accomplished by the work that students and instructors actually put in on writing. A book for a writing course should get in the way of that work as little as possible, and that is the sort of book we have tried to write, with the essential minimum of theory in the first part (along with some practical advice on procedures in writing and some materials for group consideration), followed by some demanding but possibly amusing exercises in the last part.

In putting this book together we have tried to make available in a straightforward and elementary way the knowledge about writing that has been developed in recent years by studies in linguistics, semantics, literary criticism, and the philosophy of language. We found we could do this best by concentrating on the sentence and the short sequence of sentences. Obviously, in any thorough study of writing, larger sequences must be attended to as well. But this book is not a guide to the whole study of writing. It is a point of departure, a first book, a book of elements.

R. S

November 1971   C. H. K.

Acknowledgments

In making this book we have had valuable advice and criticism from a number of people. Professors John F. Butler, of Drexel University, and Glen A. Love, of the University of Oregon, provided us with detailed critiques of the entire manuscript, which resulted in many changes, large and small. Richard Hootman, of the University of Iowa, and his class of Rhetoric 10:3, tested an early version of the book in the summer of 1970. This test resulted in a useful report by Professor Hootman and some helpful comments by individual students—which led us to make significant revisions.

Our editors at the Oxford University Press—George Allen and John Wright—provided assistance and encouragement for which we are most grateful. We are also grateful to all those scholars and critics, teachers and students, who have helped us to learn what we know about writing.

Contents

PART ONE
ELEMENTS OF WRITING

Writing, Speaking, and Thinking

Speaking is a natural activity for a human being. Nobody teaches us to speak. We learn without formal instruction. But writing is an *unnatural* activity. It must be taught formally and studied deliberately. And many of the problems that arise in learning to write are simply problems in finding the proper written equivalent for the materials of speech. The spelling of our words is a clumsy attempt to reproduce the sounds of our voices. The punctuation of our sentences and setting off of paragraphs is designed to give some approximation of the pauses and intonations we use automatically to give shape and point to our speaking.

The writer of English (or any other language) loses a whole world of gestures, facial expressions, and tones of voice the minute he decides to write something rather than say it out loud. He loses the immediacy of direct contact with his audience. If there were no compensations for all these disadvantages, then communicating with other people through the medium of squiggles on paper would be as unsatisfactory as trying to wash your feet with your socks on. Fortunately, there *are* compensations (even though that word *"are"* has to be printed in italic type in order to capture an intonation that would be conveyed effortlessly in speech).

Writing takes more effort than speech, but the effort we make simply to capture our words on paper can also lead us to compose things that are worth the effort. The unusual energy that goes into achievement in any art or sport can and should function finally to help the individual increase his own powers and perfect his abilities. Three hundred and fifty years ago a clever man pointed out that practice in speaking makes a man "ready" or quick in his responses, while practice in writing makes a man "exact," helps him to polish and perfect his thought.

Thinking, of course, is related to both speaking and writing. We think partly in words but also in images and moods and other wordless ways. In writing down our thoughts we face the problems of reducing this rich and complex process to a system which is purely verbal. Every time we use or want to use a picture or a chart or a diagram, we are aware of the limitations of mere writing with respect to the ideas we want to convey. But the challenge and the difficulty of reducing thought to writing can and do actually work as a stimulus; they lead us to think thoughts we would never have thunk without the discipline that writing requires. ("Thunk?" Is one permitted to think such a word? To write it? We will come back to this question.)

And the permanence of writing! The thoughts and sounds that we put into written shape will keep their form exactly. Thus every bunch of words that we collect and arrange on our pages will stay there to be compared to the next bunch. This permanence of our arrangements of words is at the center of the problems—and the opportunities—that writing offers us. In normal conversation we repeat a lot and we skip about from thought to thought. We do *not* talk in sentences and paragraphs. There is nothing wrong with this. It is ordinary verbal behavior. But what is tolerable in talk is often intolerable when reduced to writing. Because writing is permanent, it requires more control than speech. Once we put together a short arrangement of words that make sense as a group (call it a "sentence" for convenience) we have two big problems. The next one we write must be connected to the first one. That's one problem. It must also add something new to the first one. That's the other problem. A sequence of sentences must be *coherent;* and it must be *developmental.* It must stick together and it must get somewhere. If we were to continue writing the same sentence over and over again we would have wonderful coherence, perfect coherence in fact. But after a few repetitions we would not have many readers. Coherence without dvelopment is worthless. If we could produce a sequence of sentences with absolutely no relation to one another (which is quite hard, try it), then we would have the perfection of development—pure chaos, utter nonsense. Development without coherence is also worthless. All good writing, absolutely all, is both coherent and developmental.

Writing, then, is a discipline. It is a special form of soundless speech and verbal thought. To deal with any aspect of our life in writing is harder than to speak about it or to "think" about it. But after we have submitted to the discipline of writing we can return to thought and speech with a stronger command of language and therefore with a better grasp of whatever aspect of life we wish to confront. The best writers aim at producing something that will be worthy of the permanence that written language has. They would like, as John Milton put it, to leave something so written to after-times that the world will not willingly let it die. But anyone who writes on any subject, even if no other person ever sees his written words, will find that what he has written will leave its invisible marks on his further thinking and speaking on that subject.

Man is an animal that lives in language as a fish lives in water. The spoken language is our element, the most distinctive feature of our human existence. In a sense, for a man to write is as unnatural as for a fish to crawl up on the land and become amphibious. But human nature is based on such unnatural occurrences. Now man must master his language or it will master him. The ability to handle language with grace and confidence is not just a ticket to gainful employment—though it is that to some extent. It is a key to expanded perception, to fuller life. The case of language is different from other kinds of bodily and mental achievement only in that we cannot refuse it. Whether we master tennis or the guitar is something we can decide for ourselves. But imagine knowing only two or three chords and being handed a guitar by every person you met, and being told to play something. You can't hide from language. It will come after you. It is an instrument you must learn to play—and play in public.

Because writing is the most disciplined aspect of language, it is the one that can be studied most closely and perfected most thoroughly. That is why we are offering in this book ways of gaining greater command of the fundamentals of written language.

Speaking and Writing

Many problems in writing can be seen as the direct result of difficulties in transforming speech into written form. All of the so-called "mechanical" errors in writing are the result of failures to solve this kind of problem. Spelling, for instance, poses special problems because English written words are not perfect phonetic transcriptions of the sounds of English speech. Before the eighteenth century, spelling was still unsettled and everyone spelled according to his own sense of sound. Even a personal name like Shakespeare could be spelled several ways, and was by Shakespear himself. But since spelling has become settled and recorded in dictionaries, "correctness" in spelling has become a virtue and incorrect spelling a vice. Since it is one of the few matters in language which can be settled (by consulting a dictionary), it often receives undue attention. Even people who may not be able to understand or evaluate your ideas are likely to know whether or not your spelling is "correct." To judge a person's value by spelling is a bit like judging him by his clothing or the length of his hair. It is a social judgment, not an intellectual one.

What, then, should the student of writing do about spelling? First of all he should make some effort to avoid putting himself at a disadvantage. By spelling correctly he can force his readers—whether they are friends, parents, teachers, employers, or anybody else—to evaluate his writing on some less superficial principle. And this is important, because even the fairest and friendliest reader can be put off by bad spelling. As he reads he will be getting signals that say, "illiterate, illiterate" every time he finds a misspelled word; and even if he makes a conscious effort not to pay too much attention to this, he is likely—especially if he is a teacher—to resent your causing him that effort. Other readers, less friendly, may even use spelling errors or obvious mistakes in grammar and punctuation as a way of discrediting any ideas you present. Lack of conformity in matters as social as spelling and grammar constitutes a kind of challenge to the linguistic establishment. This doesn't automatically turn every bad speller into a revolutionary, but it may make him suspect in the eyes of people who make social judgments on the basis of language. And many people—perhaps most people—do just that. So if you want to be a nonconformist in these matters, do it with the awareness that there will be social consequences. And remember that even the most radical of revolutionaries have not yet begun to insist on "free spelling for a free people."

Until the day of total freedom in the global village arrives, there will be good reason to attain a reasonable correctness in spelling. But how? That is the question. Some people have little difficulty with spelling while others have a lot; but good and bad spellers are not necessarily the same as good and bad writers. If you are a really bad speller, you have a special problem. There are whole books devoted to this problem and useful exercises that can be undertaken. A teacher's guidance is what you need here— *if* you are willing to make some effort. Otherwise, forget it and prepare to suffer the consequences. But if you are among the majority of people who can spell pretty well if they care to, and often have a sense of when they need to look up a word, you have a different problem. And this problem is related to all other problems with elementary errors in grammar. In the next few pages we will try to give some practical advice for dealing with spelling and these related problems.

To eliminate these errors absolutely should be your goal, though if you come close to that ideal you will probably have done enough. The question is how to proceed. It is hard to look at our own words and see what we have actually written rather than what we had intended to write. This is not just true of spelling, it is true of every aspect of writing and of other parts of living as well. The problem is psychological. We have good intentions, and we are so close to ourselves that we assume the intentions have been carried out. We see what we want to see. With respect to writing, at least, the problem of discovering errors and failures is a problem of detachment. If we had enough knowledge and enough detachment we would never need a teacher for anything. It is because teachers can bring a more knowledgable and a more detached eye to our work that we need them. And of these two qualities detachment is probably the most important. A professional writer, who is an expert on his subject, can get very useful advice from an editor—even if the editor is not especially knowledgable on this subject—simply because the editor is detached. It is not his own work he is reading, so it is much easier for him to be critical.

The writer, then, should try to achieve a detached perspective and become the editor of his own work. To a certain extent, this *can* be managed by any of us, and there are some procedures that will help. Typing itself is useful in this way. Because the machine comes between us and our writing we can see our errors and difficulties more clearly than if we have to search for them through our own familiar handwriting.

Another way to achieve detachment is to use time. If you read something just after you have written it, you are much less likely to get a critical perspective on it than if you put it aside for a while. The cold light of early morning is especially appropriate for editing prose produced by midnight brainstorms, but the longer you can let something sit, the more detached your perspective can be. This, of course, means planning ahead so as to allow time for editing.

Yet another way to achieve editorial distance is to introduce a device like a ruler or blank four-by-six card into the process, so that you are forced to slow down and read line by line, not moving the card or ruler until you are satisfied that each line is clean. (This means that you will not be so sensitive to problems of continuity, so that you should proofread at least twice, using different speeds.)

It should be obvious that these remarks about the value of editing do not apply merely to spelling but to every aspect of writing. Everything you *know* about writing can be brought to bear during your editorial self-scrutiny. Granted, none of the editorial methods suggested here can take you beyond the limits of your ability, but the goal in writing, as in every other human activity, is not to achieve the impossible but to do one's best within limitations. And if we keep trying to reach our highest level, the level itself is likely to rise. The experience of editing your own work should finally begin to affect your writing processes themselves. You will write with a heightened awareness and, probably, write better.

Many other problems in writing are related to the problem of spelling and should be dealt with in the same way. Any person who speaks a language and understands it when it is spoken *knows* the grammar of that language. For instance, if you encountered the following utterance—"The najes have all been zartaned!"—you might be somewhat at a loss, since two of the key items are nonsense words invented for this occasion, but you would still know a surprising amount about what had been said. You would know (1) that the utterance is a statement, not a question, (2) that it is, in fact, an emphatic statement or exclamation, and (3) that it is a complete sentence. If you heard it aloud, the intonation pattern of the speaker's voice would confirm all these things. Reading it, you must rely on the punctuation to give you a clue to the intonation. Consider this dialogue:

Frank: The najes have all been zartaned!
Ernest: The najes have all been zartaned?
Frank: The najes have all been zartaned.

The capital letters at the beginning of each utterance signal the start of a sentence. The three different marks of punctuation at the end of each sentence signal three different kinds of intonation. If you were to read any of these sentences aloud with the appropriate intonation, your listeners would certainly know which one you had read. But you know more about these three sentences than we have yet considered. You know (1) that "najes" must be things and (2) that "zartaned" must be some action or process that has been completed. How do you know these things? Your sense of grammar, developed through years of using English, told you. The *s* on the end of "najes" and the *ed* on the end of "zartaned" were clues. And the way that *ed* goes with "have . . . been" is important, too. In your linguistic life you have encountered so many things that "have been" this-*ed* and "have been" that-*ed* that you recognize the grammatical pattern instantly in this nonsense version of it, whether or not you know that it is called the past participle of a verb. You don't need the name for it to understand it. Similarly, "all" and "The" work with the *s* on "najes" to establish a pattern in which "najes" must be a plural noun. And these two patterns together establish the basic pattern of an English sentence: thing and process, noun and verb, "najes" and "zartaned."

The point of all this is that you *know* your grammar already. When you make grammatical blunders in writing—like failing to make subject and verb agree, or confusing the tenses of verbs in a sequence of sentences—it is not because you didn't know how to do it right but because you weren't paying enough attention. This can happen to us when we wander into sentence structures that are more extended or more complicated than the kind we use in speech. The remedies for this are simple. We must either stick close to the simple structures we have learned to manage orally, or we must learn to pay attention more carefully to what we are doing when we generate an extended or complicated sentence. If, for example, we drift into a long sentence, full of items that interrupt the flow, some of which are relative clauses which have within them other relative clauses and parenthetical remarks—like this one—that distract our attention from the fact that we began with an "if" which requires a "then" before the structure can be completed, then we must not forget how we have started or abandon our structure in the middle from confusion, forgetting that a sentence with an "if" and a "then" may well need a "but" before it can complete itself comfortably, but we must persevere, concentrating intently, holding the thought in our head and our breath in our lungs, while we race furiously toward that blissful moment when we can conclude with that perfect and appropriate mark of punctuation: the period. There. Was it worth it? Sometimes it is. Sometimes the complexity of our thought can be accommodated only in a complex sentence, but often it is neither necessary nor desirable. Every deviation from simplicity and directness must be justified in two ways: first by your ability to sustain your grammar over the long haul, and second by the necessity for a complex sentence at that moment in your thinking. Once you get beyond the most elementary matters in writing there are no rules to follow. In a sense, whatever works is right. Even a totally non-standard item of usage, like "thunk" (see p. 4), which does not usually appear in dictionaries, can be useful if it will be understood and effective in its context.

Dictionaries, of course, are strange and wonderful things. They are consulted most often by people who want to know the accepted spelling of a particular word. Which is curious because you cannot find a word in the dictionary except by the way it is spelled. If you really have no idea how to spell a word, you can't begin to look it up. In practice most of us make a guess and try it out, guessing again and again until we find the right spelling. In addition to giving us accepted spellings, dictionaries do give us us defi-nitions and comments on the usage of words. A good dic-tionary will discriminate among so-called "synonyms," illustrating the fine distinctions in usage which prevent synonyms from "meaning" the same thing.

The meaning of words, however, is not entirely a matter of dictionary definition. Far from it. This complex subject will be treated in the next chapter, but before getting deeper into theoretical matters, we would like you to pause and consider item M1. (The "M" stands for "Materials for Group Consideration." After most of these theoretical chapters we will provide M's to help readers get a grip on the ideas and techniques discussed in each chapter. These are not meant to be assignments or tests of individual comprehension so much as ways of reconsidering certain matters and talking over problems and questions that arise out of such consideration. A room equipped with blackboard, chalk, teacher, etc., will probably serve very well for this sort of discussion.) M1 is designed to lead into some of the problems that will be raised in the next chapter as well as to emphasize the aspects of writing we have just been discussing.

M1

The following paragraphs are from the opening pages of a novel by Anthony Burgess called *A Clockwork Orange*. The novel is set in slightly future time and told by a teenage hoodlum in a lively kind of slang used only by people his own age. The reader is expected to pick up an understanding of this *slanguage* as he goes along. In reading this material, underline all the words that are not standard expressions.

'What's it going to be then, eh?'

There was me, that is Alex, and my three droogs, that is Pete, Georgie, and Dim, Dim being really dim, and we sat in the Korova Milkbar making up our rassoodocks what to do with the evening, a flip dark chill winter bastard though dry. The Korova Milkbar was a milk-plus mesto, and you may, O my brothers, have forgotten what these mestos were like, things changing so skorry these days and everybody very quick to forget, newspapers not being read much neither. Well, what they sold there was milk plus something else. They had no licence for selling liquor, but there was no law yet against prodding some of the new veshches which they used to put into the old moloko, so you could peet it with vellocet or synthemesc or drencrom or one or two other veshches which would give you a nice quiet horrorshow fifteen minutes admiring Bog And All His Holy Angels And Saints in your left shoe with lights bursting all over your mozg. Or you could peet milk with knives in it, as we used to say, and this would sharpen you up and make you ready for a bit of dirty twenty-to-one, and that was what we were peeting this evening I'm starting off the story with.

Our pockets were full of deng, so there was no real need from the point of view of crasting any more pretty polly to tolchock some old veck in an alley and viddy him swim in his blood while we counted the takings and divided by four, nor to do the ultra-violent on some shivering starry grey-haired ptitsa in a shop and go smecking off with the till's guts. But, as they say, money isn't everything.

1. Make a list of all the non-standard words that you have underlined. If you disagree about a particular item, see what you can devise to settle the question of whether it is "standard" or not.

2. For each item on your list, determine what part of speech it is—noun, verb, adjective, etc.

3. Consider your methods for arriving at answers for (2).

4. Try to arrive at a precise meaning for each item. Skip a word and come back to it if you get stuck.

5. Consider your methods for arriving at a meaning.
   a. How much depends on grammar?

    b.   on position in sentence?

    c.   on the word itself?

    d.   on its resemblance to other words?

    e.   on the meaning of the rest of the sentence in which it appears?

    f.   on the meaning of other sentences?

    g.   on your sense of the speaker as a person?

    h.   on something else?

6.   What conclusions about the meaning of words can you reach on the basis of your investigation of this passage?

Thinking and Writing

We think partly in words, but also in images, attitudes, sensations. If a person thinks of an image of a powerful animal, say a bull, charging at him, he can imagine the bull's color, its odor, its power, its violence, his own fear, and his own desire to flee, along with many other things—all without recourse to words like "bull," "violence," "fear," etc. But to describe this image he will have to resort to language for the image itself and for all the sensations and emotions that go along with it. If, on the other hand, he wants to think about "democracy" or "faith," he can hardly do so without those specific words and many others that describe aspects of the abstractions "democracy" and "faith." Language *can* be used to present concrete images like the charging bull; but language *must* be used to present abstractions like democracy. From this illustration it can be seen that language has a built-in tendency toward abstraction. It is a symbol system that gives names to things and arranges those names in meaningful ways. And once a person has learned his language, that system he has learned affects his perception of the images he perceives. People who use different languages actually "see" different colors around them because their words for color refer to different parts of the spectrum, arbitrarily. Every language system shapes the thinking of those who use it.

Writing is an especially powerful way of shaping thought, because it is very systematic. Thus, when a writer like James Joyce tries to represent the flow of thought or "stream of consciousness," he does so by eliminating much of the order and system we expect to find in writing, including the punctuation marks:

> . . . and the bugs tons of them at night and the mosquito nets I couldnt read a line Lord how long ago it seems centuries of course they never come back and she didnt put her right address on it either she may have noticed her wogger people were always going away and we never I remember that day with the waves and the boats with their high heads rocking and the swell of the ship those officers uniforms on shore leave made me seasick he didn't say anything he was very serious I had the high buttoned boots on I was very serious . . .   *Ulysses, p. 756*

To "make sense" of this writing we must mentally supply punctuation, add missing words, guess at the reference of pronouns, and even rearrange whole phrases; in short we must generate the elements of grammar and syntax that are missing. But even here there is enough of the structure of English as we know it to allow us to complete that structure with a fair degree of certainty. (You might try rewriting this in "prose" as an exercise.) Actual thought is probably much less verbal than this and much more jumbled. But when we think for communication—in order to speak or to write—our sense of English structure begins to take over and shape our thought. For the writer, the problem then becomes one of completing this process: finishing the thought mentally and capturing the whole structure of it in writing. This does not mean finishing the thought and *then* writing it down. There is an interaction between thought and writing. The more one develops a given thought or sequence of thought in writing, the more writing exerts a shaping pressure on the thinking process itself. This interaction takes place in every sentence, and in every sequence of sentences. But the most crucial unit of verbal thought is the individual sentence itself.

If we understand how an English sentence works, we understand the fundamental processes of our language. We have often been told that a sentence is a "complete thought." But what is a "complete thought"? A complete thought is a sentence, that's what. The definition is perfectly circular and would be utter nonsense if we did not already have in our minds a real grasp of what a sentence is. Fortunately, we *do* know. When we talk, we indicate the completeness of an utterance by the pattern of our intonation and a pause in our flow of sounds. When we write, we use certain accepted (though arbitrary) ways of signalling completeness through marks of punctuation: the period, the question mark, and so on. But what is it that we have completed? What kind of "thought" makes a sentence?

We can visualize the process of sentence construction more clearly if we imagine it as being done by a rather clumsy computer instead of by the human brain. We can call this computer a grammar machine, and imagine that it has been programed with all of the procedures which govern the writing of English. It can spell; it knows how to make nouns and verbs agree, and how to form all the tenses, moods, and voices that we have in English. Let us also assume that it can't make any "mistakes." This sounds wonderful but there is a terrible price involved. If it can't make mistakes it can't be creative—it can't change the language by inventing a new way of using it. It is limited to what is already programed into it.

Now this grammar machine has two special parts. One is a dictionary or lexicon, in which are stored all the words of our language together with their meanings. This is the *lexical* part of the grammar machine. The other part contains all the ways of combining words and arranging them. This is the *syntactical* part of the machine. It makes sure that the words the machine prints out are arranged in sentences according to the system of English syntax. To use the machine, we put in an idea or image, and the lexical part of the machine selects out all the possible words that can be used to convey this idea or image. These words are then fed into the syntactical part of the machine, which prints out all the possible arrangements of words that convey the idea or image in standard English. From this print-out, we select the best arrangement, the sentence closest to what we wanted in the first place. And if it isn't what we wanted, or isn't close enough, we have a problem. Maybe our original idea wasn't clear enough. Or maybe there is something wrong with our grammar machine.

Actually, no two of us have quite the same model of the machine. We are all programed with English, more or less effectively, but some of us have bigger and faster lexical suppliers, along with more sophisticated syntactical constructors. In the course of education, we keep trading in our little old grammar machines for larger new ones. Some get broken, and some get rusty from lack of use, but a full-size grammar machine in good condition is a thing of beauty and worth all the work it takes to get it and maintain it.

And remember, our brains are much better with language than any machines that are likely to be invented for quite some time. And we can make creative "mistakes" as well as errors. The concept of a grammar machine with lexical and syntactic parts is really a very crude way of thinking about the complexities of language. (It doesn't take into account, for instance, the problem of how the original idea gets put into the machine without appearing in the form of language.) We can get a little deeper into the way language works by considering carefully some very simple sentences. Like this one:

1.   Me Tarzan, you Jane.

Considered from the lexical point of view, each of the words in the sentence has a meaning of its own, apart from the others. If you look "me" up in a dictionary, for instance, you will find that it is a form of "I"—or that both "I" and "me" are forms of the first person pronoun. "Me" is one of the sounds a person can make when he wants to refer to himself. "Tarzan," on the other hand, is one of those rare words that has a very limited meaning. There is only one Tarzan, and the word is his name. There are many Janes, of course, but in the presumed circumstances in which Tarzan says these words there is only one Jane within earshot. The word "you," like "me," has a meaning that can be looked up. It is part of our general store of language. Thus, each of the four words in this sentence has a lexical meaning.

There is also meaning in the arrangement of these four words. This is structural or syntactic meaning. If we try a few rearrangements, what do we get?

1a.   Tarzan me, Jane you.
                    (same meaning?)
1b.   You Tarzan, me Jane.
                    (different meaning)
1c.   You me, Tarzan Jane.
                    (loss of meaning, confusion, nonsense)

The arrangement affects the meaning. The act of making a sentence consists of combining bits of meaning in a meaningful way. The syntactic meaning of this sentence (in its original form) actually includes at least four little sub-sentences in its structure: (1) I have a name. (2) It is Tarzan. (3) You have a name. (4) It is Jane. Our sense of English grammar enables us to comprehend the meaning of these four sub-sentences in that original sentence. It also enables us to extract other meanings from the sentence, which differs from standard English in certain ways. The verbs are all missing, for instance, and have to be supplied. A more normal way to make this utterance might be "I'm Tarzan and you're Jane."—with the verbs supplied in the form of " 'm" and " 're," which we recognize as forms of "am" and "are." In the revised, "normal" form of the sentence we have also changed "Me" to "I." The original, verbless sentence and the use of "me" combine to suggest a speaker whose command of English is rudimentary. Our sense of grammar suggests a context for the sentence which extends beyond itself. This particular sentence suggests very strongly a context which is partly verbal and partly dramatic. And here we must pause and examine the notion of *context*.

As we are going to use the word, *context* means the immediate surroundings of any given sentence. The verbal context is made up of the other sentences which surround it. The dramatic context is made up of our sense of the person who has uttered the sentence and the person or persons who perceive it. In the sample sentence a person called Tarzan is speaking to a person called Jane. But if we were to read that sentence in a Tarzan story, this simple dramatic context would be complicated by the fact that we would also have in that sentence and every other sentence a person (the author) who is addressing another person (the reader) *through* the speech of Tarzan to Jane. In this instance he would be saying to us that Tarzan is a simple fellow who speaks simply. (In the actual Tarzan books, as a matter of fact, Tarzan is an English Lord who can speak beautifully if he feels like it. It is the movie Tarzan whose character is reflected in the sample sentence.)

In its full verbal context, the sentence would also have a fuller dramatic context, and might carry certain implied meanings such as "Pleased to meet you" or "Let's get to know one another better" or "You have a name too, and it's Jane, and now we can call one another by name, Wow! that's wonderful." If the words were said in a movie, the *way* they were said and the listener's reaction to them might convey even more meaning than the arrangement of words itself. Tarzan's tone of voice, his gestures, the way Jane listened—all these things could affect the meaning significantly. Similarly, some of this dramatic context might be presented in the verbal context of the sentence. Consider these variations:

1d.   "Me Tarzan, you Jane," he said roughly.

1e.   "Me Tarzan, you Jane," he said tenderly.

1f.   "Me Tarzan, you Jane," he said lustfully.

Thus far, we have three kinds of meaning to consider, each one including its predecessors: *lexical*, *syntactic*, and *contexual*. And there is a fourth, which is equally important and contains all the others.

Suppose a man were to walk up to a sweet young thing at a party and say, "Me Tarzan, you Jane." What would this mean? If the sweet young thing had never heard of Tarzan, it would not mean very much to her, except that someone was trying a new line. A kind of dramatic meaning would have been conveyed, even so, but certainly not the full meaning, for the full meaning depends on her ability to recognize the allusion. She must be able to take the expression from its original context and see how it relates to this new one. To do this she must impose an image of that simple jungle scene on the civilized one in which she is standing and listening to the expression. In doing this, she will recognize certain similarities and be aware of certain differences in the two contexts. A man is speaking to a woman in both situations, and speaking to her for the first time, probably. But a civilized party is a long way from Tarzan's jungle. (Or is it? Some things are basic.)

In another new context, as an allusion, the sentence will take on different meanings depending on exactly who says it and who hears it. If a big powerful man says it to a sweet little thing—one kind of meaning. But suppose a ninety-eight-pound weakling says it to a great Valkyrie of a female: the meaning changes, doesn't it? It becomes less straightforward, more ironic, funnier.

And notice what we did a couple of sentences back. We brought two additional contexts to bear on the situation: the ninety-eight-pound weakling comes from the advertisements for Charles Atlas's muscle-building program. In these ads, the weakling often loses his girl friends to well-built types until he builds his own muscles. Thus the connection to Tarzan is appropriate. And Valkyries are the mythological females who were supposed to carry the bodies of dead heroes to the heavenly Valhalla in Norse mythology. In Grand Opera they have often been portrayed by women of heroic stature. Somewhere deep in this complicated group of allusions the images of Tarzan, carrying

Jane over his shoulder to his jungle bower, and an operatic Valkyrie with a dead hero slung across her saddle, are allowed to merge and interact.

This fourth level of meaning can be called *allusive*. Allusive meaning brings other contexts than the immediate one to bear on any given sentence. Achievement in writing can be seen in terms of the four levels that we have been considering. The best writers are those who exert the most control over all four levels. They have the greatest sense of the lexical fit between words and things, the greatest facility in finding syntactic patterns appropriate to their thoughts, the firmest grasp of the total context of each sentence they write, and the richest and most vigorous sense of the allusive possibilities of their language. Just as anyone can learn the moves well enough to play chess but only a master can see far enough ahead and hold enough possibilities in his mind to play really well, so we can all learn the necessary minimum of lexical and syntactical rules to write but only a master can write so well that people want to go on reading his work year after year. There is, of course, a great range of achievement possible between the work of the grand masters of writing and the minimally literate. And somewhere on that scale each of us takes his place: a place partly determined by innate ability but finally settled according to achievement, not potential.

Assuming a person who wants to write up to his potential, how does he do it? He does it by reading and writing. By seeing how others have done it and by doing it himself. The questions that arise then are what he should read and what he should write. Clearly, he should read those writers whose work has been good enough to endure. Among the people whose writing has been good enough to endure are the poets. In poetry, we frequently find writing in which the greatest possible attention has been paid to context and allusiveness. Poetry draws much of its power from its use of metaphor and irony, and these are but two dimensions of allusiveness in writing. Metaphor is a structure of comparison which enriches context in an allusive way, by bringing an image from outside the immediate context into that context. If a person says, "I hate Tarzan because he always barks at me," he is using metaphor to bring the image of a dog into the context of his attitude toward Tarzan. Irony, on the other hand, is a structure of contrast which enriches context by displacing something expected with something unexpected. If a person says, "Tarzan is a terrific tennis player; Jane has to work pretty hard every now and then to keep him from winning a game"—we have irony because the word "terrific" becomes inappropriate as the sentence moves toward its conclusion. This is verbal irony of a simple sort, but there is situational or dramatic irony here as well, because we expect great athletic feats from Tarzan, and in this case our expectations are comically disappointed.

The following materials are designed to focus on the lexical, syntactic, contextual, and allusive problems we have been considering in this chapter. Before turning to these new materials, however, it might be useful to reconsider M1 from these four points of view. In your discussion of M1, what sort of lexical, syntactic, contextual, and allusive problems did you encounter? In what ways did you use each of these four aspects of meaning to help you understand the others?

M2

The following two passages were both written by Ernest Hemingway. Item A was part of a cable he sent to his newspaper while he was working as a war correspondent in Turkey during the fall of 1922. Item B was written in the summer of 1923.

A.   In a never-ending, staggering march the Christian population of Eastern Thrace is jamming the roads towards Macedonia. The main column crossing the Maritza River at Adrianople is twenty miles long. Twenty miles of carts drawn by cows, bullocks and muddy-flanked water buffalo, with exhausted, staggering men, women and children, blankets over their heads, walking blindly in the rain beside their worldly goods.

This main stream is being swelled from all the back country. They don't know where they are going. They left their farms, villages and ripe, brown fields and joined the main stream of refugees when they heard the Turk was coming. Now they can only keep their places in the ghastly procession while mud-splashed Greek cavalry herd them along like cow-punchers driving steers.

It is a silent procession. Nobody even grunts. It is all they can do to keep moving. Their brilliant peasant costumes are soaked and draggled. Chickens dangle by their feet from the carts. Calves nuzzle at the draught cattle wherever a jam halts the stream. An old man marches bent under a young pig, a scythe and a gun, with a chicken tied to his scythe. A husband spreads a blanket over a woman in labor in one of the carts to keep off the driving rain. She is the only person making a sound. Her little daughter looks at her in horror and begins to cry. And the procession keeps moving.

B.   Minarets stuck up in the rain out of Adrianople across the mud flats. The carts were jammed for thirty miles along the Karagatch road. Water buffalo and cattle were hauling carts through the mud. No end and no beginning. Just carts loaded with everything they owned. The old men and women, soaked through, walked along keeping the cattle moving. The Maritza was running yellow almost up to the bridge. Carts were jammed solid on the bridge with camels bobbing along through them. Greek cavalry herded along the procession. Women and kids were in the carts crouched with mattresses, mirrors, sewing machines, bundles. There was a woman having a kid with a young girl holding a blanket over her and crying. Scared sick looking at it. It rained all through the evacuation.

1.   How, in general, would you describe the relationship between the two pieces?

2.   How many different kinds of general relationship seem important?

3.   List the important lexical differences between the two pieces.

4.   Does your list of lexical differences enable you to say anything about the pattern of lexical changes, or the principles that seem to have been governing the lexical revision?

5.   List the important grammatical and syntactic changes.

6.   What does this new list enable you to conclude about the method of revision?

7.   Which do you think were more significant—the lexical revisions or the changes in grammar and syntax?

8.   Item A was a work of journalism, written for a news-

paper. Item B was included as an "interchapter" between two stories in a volume of fiction called *In Our Time*. Thus the total context for A was journalistic and for B was fictional.

a. Does this affect your reading of the two pieces?

b. Do you feel one is truer or realler than the other?

c. Is one more "effective" than the other?

d. Is one "better" than the other?

e. Do they say the same thing?

M3

Item A and item B are passages from a book about boxing called *The Sweet Science*, by A. J. Liebling.

A. Most of the sports writers in the papers seemed to take roughly my view of the probabilities, although they phrased them more elegantly than I would have thought possible before I boarded the plane. "Bald on top but smart inside, old Jersey Joe Walcott is razor sharp and ready to shear boxing's gold-crusted heavyweight crown off champion Rocky Marciano's proud, unbowed head tonight at the Chicago Stadium," a figure-of-speech man named Wendell Smith, of the Chicago *American*, began his piece. "The most amazing, durable antique in the museum of mayhem, the thirty-nine-year-old challenger intends to cut the rugged champion down with his slashing, powerful tools of destruction as quickly as possible and become the first fighter in history to regain the heavyweight title. Tradition says he can't do it. Seven others have had the same opportunity and failed. The gods of chance are against him, too. They've made old Joe the 3-1 underdog. They're heaping their affections and blessings on the young man—the bull-like kind of clout from Brockton, Mass., who strikes with the terrifying might of Thor and the lightning suddenness of Ajax. The experts, too, believe Walcott is about to be sacrificed upon the altar of futility." This was just about the way I saw things.

1. First consider only the long quotations from Wendell Smith, ignoring Liebling's own words.

   a. Make a list of Smith's allusions and metaphors. (If you have difficulty deciding whether some things are metaphors or not, don't be surprised. You may want to take time out to develop a definition beyond the one given on p. 26. And you may want to distinguish between a simple metaphor and a metaphor which is extended or complicated in some way. Go ahead. Time spent in understanding metaphor will not be wasted.)

   b. Using the list you have compiled, and considering the whole of Smith's statement, how successful do you feel he has been in using metaphor?

2. Now consider the material in A which is not by Smith but by the book's author, Liebling: that is, the first sentence, part of the second, and the last.

   a. What do you take to be Liebling's attitude toward Smith?

   b. What evidence in the text supports your answer to 2a?

   c. To what extent is Liebling an ironist?

3. Taking the whole passage together, how do the Liebling parts and the Smith parts work to form a context?

B.   "Sweet Science of Bruising!"
                                      Boxiana, 1824

> "I had heard that Ketchel's dynamic onslaught was
> such it could not readily be withstood, but I figured
> I could jab his puss off. . . . I should have put the
> bum away early, but my timing was a fraction of an
> iota off."
>
> —*Philadelphia Jack O'Brien*, talking in 1938
> about something that had happened long ago.

It is through Jack O'Brien, the *Arbiter Elegantium Phila-
delphiae*, that I trace my rapport with the historic past
through the laying-on of hands. He hit me, for pedagogi-
cal example, and he had been hit by the great Bob Fitzsimmons, from whom he won the light-heavyweight title
in 1906. Jack had a scar to show for it. Fitzsimmons had
been hit by Corbett, Corbett by John L. Sullivan, he by
Paddy Ryan, with the bare knuckles, and Ryan by Joe
Goss, his predecessor, who as a young man had felt the
fist of the great Jem Mace. It is a great thrill to feel that
all that separates you from the early Victorians is a series
of punches on the nose. I wonder if Professor Toynbee is
as intimately attuned to his sources. The Sweet Science is
joined onto the past like a man's arm to his shoulder.

The quotation from *Boxiana* and the one from Jack O'Brien,
along with the paragraph that follows them, make up the
first page of Liebling's book.

1.   First consider the quotation from O'Brien. He seems to
     be mixing his lexical levels, using some elaborate words
     and some very plain ones. What is the effect of this
     mixed context?

2.   Looking at Liebling's own first paragraph, be sure you
     understand his allusions.

    a.   What is "the laying-on of hands"—that is, what is the traditional meaning of this expression?

    b.   How does this allusion function in its context?

    c.   And the allusion to Toynbee?

3.   How do you interpret a phrase like "intimately attuned"? In what ways does it fit the Toynbee context and the O'Brien-Liebling context?

4.   Consider the simile in the last sentence. (A simile is a kind of metaphoric comparison, introduced by "like" or "as," etc.) How does this metaphor function in the whole context?

5.   What light does B throw on A?

6.   The little quotation from *Boxiana*. Is it metaphorical? Ironic? What?

The Shape of Written Thought: Sentences

How does an English sentence work? At the very simplest level, creating a sentence involves selecting the name of a thing (a single noun or substantive word) and selecting another word which tells us something about that thing. This "telling us something" is usually called "modifying," or changing, the noun. Thus instead of saying just "Me," someone says, "Me Tarzan." The modification is a matter of connecting that first noun with one or more other words. When this modification takes a syntactic shape satisfying certain conditions, we call it predication, and we recognize the finished product as a sentence. We can begin the study of predication by returning to the simple sentence we began with in the last chapter, this time taking only a part of it, for even greater simplicity. But watch closely. Things will be getting complicated soon enough.

PREDICATION

1.   Me Tarzan.

In this structure the word "Tarzan" is added to the word "me," altering or modifying it. Here are some other sentences constructed on the same plan:

2. Me boss.

3. Me happy.

In sentence 2 we added a noun to "Me"; in sentence 3, an adjective; but this made no essential difference to the structure of the sentence. The difference is purely lexical—it is in the meaning of the words. Structurally, each word simply added to our knowledge of the first. Now consider two variations on these sentences:

2a. Tarzan boss

3a. Tarzan happy.

Here we have substituted "Tarzan" for "me," but the structure is the same, the first noun modified by the noun or adjective added to it. Now consider these variations:

2b. Tarzan is boss.

3b. Tarzan is happy.

Here we have supplied a verb which links the two elements that originally composed each sentence. Does the verb change the meaning? Not really. Well then, what does it do? It gives verbal form to that notion of linkage which was previously present only by implication. It realizes more of the structure of the sentence, making it concretely available to the reader. The phrases "is boss" and "is happy" are now recognizable as examples of the "predicate" of a standard English sentence, a verb plus something else. But the something else is the crucial thing, the verb is a convenience. Now consider these two new sentences:

4. Tarzan loves Jane.

5. Tarzan walks slowly.

Here the verbs seem to be more important, because they

are not merely linking verbs but are action verbs, themselves capable of sustaining the weight of a sentence without the additional word that follows them, as in

4a. Tarzan loves.

5a. Tarzan walks.

Yet even these sentences can be reduced to a more elementary form:

4b. Tarzan is (a) lover.

5b. Tarzan is (a) walker.

or even to the most elementary form:

4c. Tarzan lover.

5c. Tarzan walker.

A language without verbs is possible. We could even reconstruct the whole sentences we began with in verbless form:

4d. Tarzan Jane-lover.

5d. Tarzan slow-walker.

What then is the difference between (4d) "Tarzan Jane-lover" and (4) "Tarzan loves Jane"? There are several differences. Clearly "Tarzan loves Jane" is the normal way of stating the idea in English. It is more "correct." It is also more dynamic because it puts the active emotion, love, in the form of the active verb. Predication with no verb is possible, but it is clumsy and not normal in English. Predication with a linking verb is perfectly normal—(4e) Tarzan is in love with Jane—but less compact and vigorous than predication with an active verb—(4) Tarzan loves Jane.

In English we use linking verbs (especially "is," "are," and other forms of the verb "to be") with great frequency.

They function effectively in much of our writing and thinking. But we also have a tendency to overuse them. We
sometimes fail to generate sentences with the action in the
form of an active verb when this would be the clearest and
most vigorous way to express our intention. And we frequently fall into a pattern which enables us to construct
sentences with a minimum of predication, a pattern that
begins with the expression "There is" or "There are." Consider this sentence:

6.   There was a fight.

This is a perfectly grammatical English sentence, but it
predicates very little. The fight, which is the real subject of
the sentence, is not really modified by the rest of the sentence. The sentence, in fact, leads us on, causes us to desire
more information through its very vagueness. This can be
a useful device in writing (especially in narration) but only
if we use a second sentence to supply a true predicate for
this one such as,

6a.   There was a fight. The fight was between Jane and Tarzan.

In the second sentence the linking verb "was" connects the
subject to an informational predicate. Of course, all this
could have been done in a single sentence:

6b.   There was a fight between Jane and Tarzan.

And this, of course, could be expressed more energetically:

6c.   Tarzan fought Jane.

6d.   Jane fought Tarzan.

6e.   Tarzan and Jane were fighting.

6f.   Tarzan and Jane fought (one another).

6g.   Tarzan and Jane had a fight.

But 6c and 6d don't really catch the idea being presented, and, while 6e and 6f are more like it, 6g is closest to normal usage for conveying what happened here (apparently) between Tarzan and Jane. The predication "had a fight" is a complex idiom for a quarrel between two people or more. It is quite precise, yet it leaves open such questions as whether the fight was physical or verbal, which party was responsible, who won, and so on.

Now consider this variant:

6h.   Jane picked a fight with Tarzan.

This sentence not only conveys the fact that a fight was had and that Tarzan and Jane had it; it also locates the responsibility for the fight. In short, it predicates more than any other version of the sentence. It is not a more complicated structure than many of the other versions. In fact it is the same simple structure that we had in 6d, but the new verbal element ("picked a fight with") does more work than the old ("fought"). This is so not because it uses four words as opposed to one; a single word like "assaulted" or "attacked" would also have predicated more than "fought"—but it would not have suited the domestic context of this quarrel as well as the four-word verbal construction that we actually used. Sentence 6h is more alive, more vigorous than the other versions, because it compacts more meaning into that same simple structure. It is not, of course, a model for all good sentences, but it suggests something about the usefulness of action verbs in the process of predication and about the value of action verbs which convey as much information as possible, thus strengthening the predicate. And predication, as should be obvious by now, is at the heart of sentence construction. A

sentence is a noun (or a noun phrase) successfully predicated.

Another problem in predication that often troubles
writers of English is related to the problem of excessive
reliance on linking verbs and feeble constructions that
begin with "There is" and "There are." This problem involves excessive use of passive verbs. Consider this
sentence:

7.   Jane was hit.

This is a perfectly grammatical sentence which satisfies our
desire for structural completeness. It also succeeds in giving us some information—more than we would have obtained if the sentence read

7a.   A blow was struck.

Sentences 7 and 7a are both passive constructions, but 7
conveys more information than 7a. In 7a the predication
is nearly redundant, in that the notion of a "blow" clearly
implies the notion of striking. In 7 we get sufficient predication to appease some of our hunger for information, but
not enough, really. Consider these variations on the basic
sentence:

7b.   Jane was hit by Tarzan.

7c.   Jane was hit in the nose.

7d.   Jane was hit in the nose by Tarzan.

7e.   Tarzan hit Jane.

7f.   Tarzan hit Jane in the nose.

7g.   Tarzan hit Jane in the nose, breaking it.

7h.   Tarzan broke Jane's nose.

Both 7b and 7c give us more information than 7 by expanding the predicate. Sentence 7b is, in fact, the passive

version of 7e. What distinguishes the active version of this sentence from the passive? Mainly the fact that in 7b the person doing the hitting, the agent or actor, is tacked on to the basic sentence. In the original passive version of this sentence, 7, Tarzan was not present and did not need to be present for the sentence to be complete and grammatically satisfying. But sentence 7e *requires* the presence of Jane (or some other object) to be complete. A sentence like this—

7i.   Tarzan hit

—strikes us as incomplete until an object like "Jane" is added to the predicate. The active form *demands* more thorough predication than the passive. And the three words of sentence 7e convey much more information than the three words of sentence 7.

Similarly, in sentence 7f the added phrase "in the nose" is not necessary to complete the structure of the sentence, and in 7g both the phrases in the predicate, which convey important information, are simply added on to the basic structure rather than included in that structure. But in 7h every word is necessary to complete the structure. (It would be possible to say "Tarzan broke Jane," but it is not normal and it would not convey the meaning intended here.) The word "Tarzan" needs some predication to become a sentence. "Tarzan broke" requires an object to complete the active form of the verb. (Compare "Jane's nose was broken.") And at this point we can see that neither of the other words in the sentence is capable of making the sentence satisfactorily complete by itself:

7j.   Tarzan broke Jane's

7k.   Tarzan broke nose

Each of these forms requires further information to complete the sentence. Coming upon 7k without a context we might make the assumption that Tarzan had broken his own nose. We would supply "his" before "nose" to complete the grammar of the sentence. But we would certainly recognize the incompleteness and feel the need to supply *some* form of possessive noun or pronoun before the word "nose." Similarly, sentence 7j would lead us inevitably to guess at or mentally supply some possession of Jane's or some part of her anatomy to complete the structure satisfactorily. The verb "broke" in this context ("Jane picked a fight with Tarzan. Tarzan broke Jane's nose.") includes the meaning of the verb "hit," includes that whole notion of a blow being struck by Tarzan at Jane, and adds to it the notion of this blow resulting in some specific form of breakage or fracture. Sentence 7h generates a higher power of predication than any of the others—through the selection of an active verb which not only requires an object but which predicates something specific about that object.

Co-ordination

Predication is the crucial operation in the construction of simple sentences. It is the most important single action we perform in writing, and the most fundamental. The action which stands next to predication in its fundamental importance is the act of connecting and combining simple sentences into larger structures. As in the operation of predicating, we have in this larger operation a hierarchy of complexity and intensity. In predicating we use either the simple linking structure (with the verb "to be" and its associated verbs of being), or a more compact structure based on action verbs. Similarly, in putting together simple sentences to make larger ones, we can either link them in a "compound" structure which allows each clause to maintain its equal or "independent" status; or we can combine them in a more compact way by subordinating one clause to the other, thus forming a "complex" sentence. In simple sentence structure we have either the linking pattern of subject, linking verb, complement; or the action pattern of subject, action verb, object. And in more complicated sentences we have either the pattern of two or more co-ordinate clauses of equal weight, or of one main clause on which one or more subordinate clauses depend. These patterns can be illustrated by using two of the Tarzan-Jane sentences we have already generated:

8. Jane picked a fight with Tarzan. Tarzan broke Jane's nose.

Once we put these sentences together like this we have already decided that the second sentence—call it 8-2—belongs after the first, 8-1. Presumably we do it this way because we think that this order represents the events we are describing more accurately than the reverse order would. On what bases might we have made that decision? Two obvious possibilities come to mind: First, the sentences follow one another in this order because the event described in 8-1 occurred *earlier in time* than the event described in 8-2. Thus the order in the writing imitates the temporal order of the action. Second, the sentences follow one another in this order because the event described in 8-1 *is the cause of* the event described in 8-2. Thus the order in the writing represents the causal relationship between the two parts of the action. For the moment, let us assume that either or both of these possibilities may be the case and that the order of the sentences is therefore appropriate. Once they are combined in this way our sense of grammar encourages us to make certain changes in them, and our care for effective writing should lead us to consider others. One simple operation that our sense of grammar encourages us to make is the substitution of pronouns for the proper names which are represented in the second sentence. Thus,

8a.   Jane picked a fight with Tarzan. He broke her nose.

This change has the effect of making the second sentence dependent on the first for parts of its meaning (lexically or semantically dependent), even though it still appears as a separate syntactic unit, beginning with a capital letter and ending with a period. Since this kind of tighter relationship among consecutive sentences is usually a desirable feature in writing, an element of coherence and development in fact, the change is a desirable one. But suppose our basic sentences were a bit different and we tried the same operation—like this:

8b.   George picked a fight with Tarzan. Tarzan broke George's nose.

8c.   George picked a fight with Tarzan. He broke his nose.

In 8a our substitution of pronouns in the second sentence worked perfectly because "He" could refer only to the man in the previous sentence and "her" could refer only to the woman. But 8c is an ambiguous recasting of 8b because it leaves us in doubt as to who broke whose nose. In fact, our grammatical instincts operate on 8c to suggest that it was George who broke Tarzan's nose, because we tend to assume that the subject of the first sentence is also the subject of the second. We impose the structure of the first on the second unless we are given some reason not to. If we really intended to convey the information that George had broken Tarzan's nose, our grammar would encourage us to combine the two sentences in this way:

8d.   George picked a fight with Tarzan and broke his nose.

In this version of the sentence, "George" becomes the subject of two parallel systems of predication governed by the verbs "picked" and "broke." There is still some ambiguity in 8d, because even though George is both the picker and the breaker, the reference of "his" is vague enough to allow us to assume that George may have broken his own nose. We could deal with this ambiguity in several ways. One would be to put "Tarzan" back in the sentence in place of "his." Another would be to substitute a phrase for "his" which would make the reference unmistakable. Like this:

8e.   George picked a fight with Tarzan and broke the poor slob's nose.

This solves the problem of pronoun reference, and also animates the sentence by the addition of a new lexical element with a strong emotional content. The sentence begins to come alive.

So much for the problems in pronoun reference that arise when we begin tightening the relationship between the two sentences. Working from version 8a, let us now consider some of the ways we might make a tighter structural connection between the two sentences, and some of the reasons that might be advanced for preferring one way to another. The simplest method of connection is to allow both sentences to remain intact as independent clauses, linked by a single connective word:

8f.   Jane picked a fight with Tarzan, and he broke her nose.

8g.   Jane picked a fight with Tarzan, but he broke her nose.

Most other connectives are merely more elaborate versions of "and" and "but." ("However" and "nevertheless" are big "buts"; "moreover" is a big "and.") Of these two connectives, "and" is the weakest. It simply adds the second element in a series to the first, without comment. But "but" comments on the relationship between the second element and the first. "But" indicates a change of direction of some sort. It requires more thought to use "but" than it does to use "and." And "but" is more dramatic; it alerts us, prepares us to look for some contrast between the two linked clauses. In examples 8f and 8g, which version is preferable? In 8f the "and" indicates that the event described in the second clause followed the event described in the first—followed in time and/or followed as an effect follows a cause. In 8g the "but" suggests a contrast which doesn't quite materialize. We do get a bit of a shift in emphasis, in that the positions of subject and object are reversed in the second clause: "Jane" is the subject of the first clause, but "her" is the object in the second. And in a way the "but" of 8g prepares us for that shift. Yet this syntactic shift is not really important enough to justify the "but." Still, it is noticeable enough to make us uneasy with "and" as the connecting link between the two clauses. Once we try to make even this simple a connection between clauses, we are led to consider revising the clauses themselves into a more dynamic relationship. Revisions along these lines begin to suggest themselves:

8h.   Jane picked a fight with Tarzan and got her nose broken.

8i.   Jane started a fight with Tarzan but he finished it by breaking her nose.

In 8h the "and" has encouraged us to make the clauses more harmonious by continuing Jane as the subject of the second clause, thus keeping our attention focused on her, actually presenting the story of these events from her point of view. Notice how this works yet other changes in the sentence:

8h-1. Jane picked a fight with Tarzan and Jane got her nose broken.

8h-2. Jane picked a fight with Tarzan and she got her nose broken.

8h. Jane picked a fight with Tarzan and got her nose broken.

In 8h-1 the subject, "Jane," is repeated in the second clause. In 8h-2 the pronoun "she" is substituted for "Jane." In the final sentence (8h) the subject is entirely eliminated from the second clause. This process, which is called *elipsis* (leaving something out), is very important in effective writing. It is natural for us to use elipsis when we generate parallel syntactic structures. Here, that single subject, "Jane," governs two parallel predicates. We can display the sentence so as to emphasize its parallel construction:

       picked a fight with Tarzan
Jane   and
       got her nose broken.

In the practical section of this book we will work extensively with such displays, because they help us to see what is actually going on in the structure of sentences. Here, for instance, because this arrangement brings the two verbs together, one below the other, it helps us to see that they are not only different words in parallel with one another, but different kinds of predication as well. The first parallel clause uses an active verbal construction; the second clause uses a passive one. There can be no confusion because the context makes it clear by implication that Tarzan must have been responsible for the damage to Jane's nose. And the shift from active to passive now effectively mirrors the shift in Jane's role in the events described. She initiated the fight—actively—and suffered the broken nose—passively. Sentence 8h is clearly an improvement on the basic sentence 8a.

Version 8i is also an improvement:

8i.   Jane started a fight with Tarzan but he finished it by breaking her nose.

The use of "but" here has been justified by a further emphasis on the shift in the subjects of the two clauses. This emphasis was achieved by adding a second verb to go with the second subject of the sentence, generating a structure which is parallel but antithetical: *Jane started* but *he finished*. The total opposition of "Jane" and "he" is reinforced by the total opposition between "started" and "finished." To achieve this antithesis, we have abstracted the meaning of "started" from the original phrase, "picked a fight with," so as to obtain that neat opposition to "finished." If we decided that we wanted to keep the less abstract and more colloquial phrase in the sentence ("picked a fight with") we could still find an appropriate antithetical verb. In fact, trying to find the right verb might lead us to enrich the sentence farther:

8j.   Jane picked a fight with Tarzan but he settled it by breaking her nose.

In this version "settled" provides a nice antithetical balance to "picked," but the word also accomplishes something else. To settle a fight is often the role of a peacemaker, who calms down the combatants. But here the fight was "settled" by the violence of one of those engaged in it.

Thus, there is a hint of irony in the word "settled." This could be developed by choosing a word which exploits even further the disparity between calm settlement and violent triumph, like this:

8k. Jane picked a fight with Tarzan, but he calmed her down by breaking her nose.

The word "calm," with its connotations of soothing peace, is ironically inappropriate to Tarzan's method of quieting Jane down. We understand that she *did* quiet down—the irony causes no confusion—but we are amused at the contrast between the peacefulness of the word and the violence of the act. Blessed are the peacemakers!

SUBORDINATION

We have been considering ways of combining two sentences into a system of co-ordinate or independent clauses. The other fundamental way of combining little sentences to make big ones is the method of subordination. Subordination requires a real act of thought, because in order to perform the action of subordinating we must determine the relative importance of the two clauses and the nature of the relationship between them. Consider these variations of the Tarzan-Jane affair:

9. Jane picked a fight with Tarzan, who broke her nose.

9a. Jane picked a fight with Tarzan, which resulted in her broken nose.

9b. Jane, who got her nose broken, picked a fight with Tarzan.

9c. When Jane picked a fight with him, Tarzan broke her nose.

9d. When she picked a fight with Tarzan, Jane got her nose broken.

The first three of these versions are rather thoughtless subordinations. In 9 "who" is substituted for "he," transforming the second half of the sentence into a modifier of Tarzan, leaving us in doubt as to whether Jane or Tarzan is the main object of our interest. Jane is the subject of the main clause, but Tarzan, through "who," is the subject of the dependent clause. The dependent clause is tacked loosely on to the sentence. Sentence 9a is similar, but "which" connects the subordinate clause to the fight (or the picking of the fight—there is some ambiguity of reference here), and "resulted" establishes a cause-and-effect relationship between the events presented in the two clauses. Still, 9a consists of a truly independent main clause, with a dependent clause loosely trailing it. We could convert 9a into two sentences by simply putting a period after "Tarzan" and changing "which" to "This." In 9b the dependent clause modifies the subject of the main clause. To achieve this modification we had to introduce the modifying clause in a position directly behind the word it modifies, thus altering the relation between the sequence of the clauses themselves and the sequence of the events narrated. In reading 9b we encounter the news of Jane's broken nose before we learn that there was a fight. There might be a reason for constructing a sentence in this way (to create suspense, for instance) but in the present case the broken nose intrudes parenthetically into a sentence which appears to be mainly about the fight. The dependent clause appears where it does, not because anyone has *chosen* to place it there but because our grammar dictates that if *this* kind of dependent clause is to appear in this sentence, it *must* go where it has been placed. Thus no decision about what the sentence is supposed to emphasize has been made in the construction of sentence 9b.

In 9c and 9d, however, we have another order of subordination, resulting in more effective sentences. In both of these cases, a decision to emphasize the result of Jane's action—the broken nose—has been made; so that the second clause of each sentence functions as the main clause. And in each case this decision has led us to move one of the proper names into the main clause, as its subject, and to substitute the appropriate pronoun for it in the dependent clause. Notice that in 9c our interest is still equally divided between Tarzan and Jane: each proper name appears once, and one pronoun refers to each name. But in 9d both of the pronouns ("she" in the dependent clause and "her" in the main clause) refer to Jane, and no pronoun refers to Tarzan. Sentence 9d is the most precisely focused of all the versions in this group. Whether it is "better" than 9c would depend on its context. Which version would be most appropriate after each of these introductory sentences?

10.   Sometimes Tarzan got rough with Jane.

10a.   Sometimes Jane suffered from Tarzan's roughness.

Clearly 9c would go best with 10 and 9d with 10a. If we put them together we would want to make some further changes in pronouns, and possibly add a connecting word.

11.   Sometimes Tarzan got rough with Jane. Once, when she picked a fight with him, he broke her nose.

In this case the connective "Once" ties the second sentence tightly to the first—specifically through its relation to "Sometimes." If we added another sentence to sequence 11 it might properly begin with such a connective as "On another occasion" or "Another time." When we build a sequence of sentences we often depend heavily on such connecting words to keep the reader aware of the pattern of thought he is following. Now consider the sequence we would make by combining 10a with 9d:

11a.   Sometimes Jane suffered from Tarzan's roughness. Once, when she picked a fight with him, she got her nose broken.

This combination works as well structurally as 11, but there is a problem in it at the level of context. If it is our intention to persuade the reader that Jane has suffered, the expression "picked a fight with" works against that intention by suggesting that she deserved what she got. For rhetorical effectiveness we would be tempted to play down the aggressiveness of her action in starting the fight, and revise the sequence in this way:

11b.   Sometimes Jane suffered from Tarzan's roughness. Once, in a family quarrel, her nose was broken.

Or we might decide that Tarzan's roughness was really the most interesting subject here—or some combination of Tarzan's roughness and Jane's suffering. This decision might lead us to add some new coloring to the basic sentences, in the form of nouns, adjectives, and adverbs. We might even suppress the "sometimes" in order to suggest that this kind of thing happened all the time.

11c.   Jane suffered terribly from Tarzan's roughness. Once in a trivial quarrel, the brute cruelly broke her lovely nose.

Here "picked a fight with" has become a "trivial quarrel" —suggesting that either of them could have started it, Tarzan being at least as guilty as Jane, and that the whole thing was a matter of no importance. Adverbs like "terribly" and "cruelly" do their work now, along with the

new noun "brute" and the adjective "lovely." We could
go further in this direction:

11d.   Jane, poor thing, suffered horribly from Tarzan's bru-
       tality. Once, for no reason at all, the beast viciously
       broke her sweet little nose.

Is this more or less effective than 9c? Is it too emotional
now, trying too hard to persuade? We begin to get a sense
of a personality behind this sequence, don't we? Consider
how 11d might function in this larger context:

12.   Cheetah writes letters about Jane's home life in the most
      exaggerated emotional language. Look at this, from her
      last: "Jane, poor thing, suffers horribly from Tarzan's bru-
      tality. Once, for no reason at all, the beast viciously broke
      her sweet little nose." So Cheetah writes. But I'd like to
      hear Tarzan's side of the story.

  Starting with predication we have got involved in matters of intensifying language, of rhetorical effectiveness,
of context and allusion, and finally, of irony. If we think
of Cheetah as human, we read sequence 12 one way. If we
remember that she is a chimpanzee, we become aware of
a complex system of ironies in front of us. Cheetah calling
Tarzan a beast has its amusing side, because she is a beast
literally, while he can be one only metaphorically. The
point of all this is that our choice of sentence construction
and our choice of verbal coloration determine our context
and are determined by our context. The whole process of
thinking in written form is a dynamic interaction between
our intentions and the sentences we generate. Intention
shapes the sentence. Each sentence affects our further intentions. If we keep our wits about us we can generate
whole sequences of written thought that are coherent and
developmental. This is a minor miracle, and one that hap-

pens to human beings every day. In the next chapter we will consider some of the basic sequences that we use in trying to extend our thought beyond the sentence.

M4

M4 is designed as a group exercise in the structuring of sentences. Its success will depend on the ingenuity of the group in exhausting the possibilities at each level of construction. Unless otherwise directed, use only the words allotted at each stage of the exercise—in exactly the given form (in other words, if "man" is given, don't use "men"; if "bites" is given, don't use "bit," etc.)

a. The importance of gesture. Let volunteers from the group try to say the single word "man" in as many different ways as they can, so that each way predicates something new about the noun "man." With an imaginative use of tone, facial expression, and gesture, members of the group should be able to generate quite a few different "sentences." Using whatever words are necessary, translate each enacted expression into a full sentence equivalent and record it. (Example: if a volunteer speaker says the word "man" while holding his nose, this might be recorded as "Man stinks!") As you get into this exercise you will discover that rather complicated notions may be conveyed through this single word. When all the possibilities are exhausted, examine your list with a view toward determining the limits of this kind of expression. How many different verbs have you been able to suggest through non-verbal means?

b. The limits of gesture. Now try taking an ordinary verb as the single word to be spoken. Pick any one you like.

What happens when you try to use gestures to supply a noun for your predicating verb? What does this tell you about the relationship between gesture and the two main parts of sentence construction—nouns and verbs?

c. Increase your list of usable words to a total of three:
   1. man
   2. dog
   3. bites

Using only the given forms of these three words, how many intelligible *written* sentences can you generate. (Use whatever punctuation is appropriate.)

d. Using each word as many times as you want, what is the longest sentence you can make with these four words:
   1. man
   2. dog
   3. bites
   4. because

e. with these four?
   1. man
   2. dog
   3. bites
   4. that

M5

a. Consider this sentence:

He loved her for her yellow hair.

Try substituting different adjectives of color in place of *yellow*. How does each substitution change the meaning of the sentence? Are some versions of the

sentence more interesting than others? What makes a
sentence like this interesting, anyway?

b. Take any one of the versions generated in a and add
    the word *but* to the end of it. Then try to complete this
    new sentence effectively *in the fewest possible words.*
    How many good possibilities are there? How much do
    they differ in structure? How much does the structure
    of the first clause affect what you can do after the *but?*
    How does the attempt to use the fewest possible words
    limit your choice of what you can possibly say?

M6

a. Let each member of the group construct a single sen-
    tence in which all the following words, appearing in
    the order given, play their appropriate structural roles.
    Use any other words that you need. You have the
    whole language to choose from. Use each one of the
    words once, and use them in the order they are given
    in. Don't just include the given words as part of a list.
    Let each one have its maximum function in structur-
    ing the sentence. And try to say something really
    meaningful within the limits we have established.

1. if	6. since
2. who	7. which
3. when	8. or
4. then	9. that
5. but	10. then

b. Consider a number of the solutions to this problem
    produced by members of the group. Select one of the
    most effective and interesting of these sentences. (You
    may well have to stop to reflect on your reasons for

finding a particular sentence effective or interesting. If so, go ahead. That's what this is all about.) Then ask the author of the sentence some of these questions:

1. How did the subject occur to you?

2. What part did the assigned list of connecting-words play in your selection of the subject?

3. What part of the sentence proved most difficult to write? Why? Easiest? Why?

4. To what extent did you have to say something you didn't want to say, in order to follow the arbitrary pattern established by the list of connecting-words?

5. Were you led to say anything you had not thought of before but consider to be true or interesting?

c. Select another successful solution to this problem and ask its author the same set of questions (and any other appropriate questions that occur to you).

d. Make up a similar exercise of your own and repeat the process with whatever variations seem appropriate.

The Shape of Written Thought: Sequences

After the sentence comes the paragraph. But what is a paragraph? A paragraph is a string of sentences. How long? Just long enough.

A paragraph is not a paragraph the way a sentence is a sentence. It does not have a necessary structure like predication. Actually, a paragraph break is simply a convenient stopping place for a train of thought, a sort of station where one can pause and then continue on the same track, switch to another, or change trains altogether if that is necessary to reach a destination. Far more interesting than paragraphs, and far more vital to the writing process, are the sequences that make them up. There are a number of recognizable kinds of sequence that we find in writing, and each kind represents a particular sort of thought process. For the rest of this chapter we will be examining some of the thought processes that operate to organize our sentences into sequences.

NARRATION

Narration is simply an arrangement of events according to time sequence. Its basic principle is that the time sequence should be followed unless there is a good reason for violating it. Consider this narrative sequence:

Jane got up. She got dressed. She made Tarzan's breakfast. He ate it. Then she made Cheetah's breakfast. Cheetah and Tarzan went out to play. Jane did the dishes and made the beds and worked very hard. Then she made lunch for Tarzan and Cheetah. Tarzan and Cheetah came home and ate lunch and went out to play again. Jane cleaned house all afternoon. Jane did not make Tarzan's dinner. Tarzan did not come home for dinner. Tarzan was dead. Jane had poisoned Tarzan's lunch.

Notice that each sentence in this sequence is itself simply narrative—subject–action-verb–object; Tarzan did this, Jane did that—until the last two sentences. The next to last sentence is descriptive. Time has stopped for Tarzan. He is out of the narrative flow. Then the very last sentence describes an event out of its natural place in the time sequence. It has been withheld for effect, to add a little surprise to the sequence. Because it has been displaced in the sequence, the tense of its verb has had to be adjusted. If the last sentence had come in its "natural" place, right after the sentence about Jane making lunch, the verb would simply be "poisoned"—the simple past. ("Jane made lunch for Tarzan and Cheetah. She poisoned Tarzan's lunch.") But because the sentence has been moved to a place in the sequence of sentences behind the place it occupies in the sequence of actions being narrated, it refers back to a past past, and the compound past tense must be used: "had poisoned." In narration, tenses can easily get confused. The writer should be careful to keep them straight.

Now consider another aspect of this sequence. What do you think of all those simple narrative sentences in a row? Are they boring? Do they have any purpose? Can you rewrite this narrative sequence so as to make it have a different effect? Can you make it better?

DESCRIPTION

As narration deals with events in time, description deals with objects in space. But since language itself is an arrangement of words in time, there is a natural temporal order for narrating events. There is no such "natural" order for describing objects. This is why a picture describes things better than words. For description in words, since there is no "natural" order, the writer must think one up. His order can be random and purposeless, like this:

On Jane's table there were a bowl, a spoon, a salt shaker, a pot of arsenic, another spoon, a napkin, another spoon, etc.

Or he can collect similar items into groupings by category, like this:

On Jane's table were thirteen items: three made of metal (spoons), four made of cloth (i.e., one tablecloth and three napkins), six made of clay (viz., three plates, one pair of salt and pepper shakers, and one pot). In the bowls there was soup. In the salt shaker, salt. In the pepper shaker, pepper. In the pot, arsenic. Also in one of the soup bowls there was some arsenic.

Or the order can be spatial, like this:

On the north side of Jane's table, the side where Cheetah once spilled some rhubarb on the tablecloth leaving a pinkish-brown stain, there were a bowl of soup, a napkin, and a spoon. On the east side. . . . On the south side. . . . On the west side. . . . And in the center there were a salt shaker, a pepper shaker, and a pot of arsenic.

In all of these descriptive passages the verbs are, of course, not verbs of action but verbs of being. Only where a narrative element intrudes into the descriptive sequence (as with Cheetah and the rhubarb) do we get an action verb ("spilled"). And no matter what principle is chosen, the order of the parts in a descriptive sequence is still fairly arbitrary. We don't *have* to go to "east" after "north," for instance, though in English we do use the order north, east, south, west a lot. If we feel that some more significant arrangement is demanded, we can try one based on the order of importance of the things being described, which means, in this case, putting the poison either first or last. As it happens, the arsenic came last in the two sample descriptions just given, which suggests that some principle of arrangement by order of importance was at work in those descriptions, even though they were meant to illustrate categorical and spatial organization rather than organization according to importance. The apparent arbitrariness of description in language always opens the door to organization according to interest or importance. Written descriptions almost inevitably turn into evaluations of one kind or another. Writing can hardly ever be really and totally neutral. But the writer always has a choice about how explicit to make his judgments. He could, for instance, emphasize the importance of the arsenic in the situation we have been describing by adding some such statement as "The most important item on Jane's table was. . . ." But judgments take us into another kind of sequential pattern, or several kinds of patterns, which we use as ways of establishing statements and convincing our readers of their rightness.

Logic

Proof is something foreign to real written language. It belongs to the world of mathematics or to special languages like that of logic. In modern symbolic logic things do not have names taken from ordinary language. Even in traditional syllogistic logic, the pure forms of thought operate best with empty categories, such as letters (A, B, C, etc.) which do not designate anything in particular. (The problem of turning such letters into words is one we will return to later.) But precisely because they operate at one of the borders of written language, the structures of logic can be useful in helping us to determine what language can and cannot accomplish in the way of proof. Let us begin by considering two of the basic syllogistic structures, expressed in the form of propositions about Tarzan and Jane:

A. All Chimpanzees love Tarzan.
    Jane loves Tarzan.
    Jane is a Chimpanzee.

B. Only chimpanzees love Tarzan.
    Jane loves Tarzan.
    Jane is a chimpanzee.

C. All women love Tarzan.
    Jane loves Tarzan.
    Jane is a woman.

D. Only women love Tarzan.
    Jane loves Tarzan.
    Jane is a woman.

In studying syllogisms we seek to determine which are valid and which are invalid. Validity is a matter of obeying the rules of thought. It should not be confused with truth. But if the two premises of a syllogism are true, and the conclusion is validly obtained from those premises, then the conclusion ought to be true also. The rules that govern the four syllogisms set forth above can be determined by the application of common sense. See if you can work them out while following the discussion in the next paragraph.

Syllogisms A and B reach the same conclusion, but A is invalid while B is valid. Neither A nor B, of course, is true. But if the major premise of B were true, and only chimpanzees really loved Tarzan, and if the minor premise were true also, and Jane really loved Tarzan, then the conclusion would be necessarily true and Jane would most certainly be a chimpanzee. The last two of these sample syllogisms reach conclusions that are true in terms of the traditional Tarzan story, but C is nevertheless invalid, while D is valid. The conclusion is not terribly useful in any case. The trouble with logic is that most of the concerns of human life do not fit into it. (How could we ever establish for sure whether Jane loved Tarzan, for instance?) Furthermore, the words of our ordinary language are so slippery that they can mean different things in different parts of the same syllogism, causing that syllogism to be apparently valid but actually invalid, without even worrying about whether the conclusion is true or not.

A certain obvious use of syllogistic patterns in persuasive writing, then, should be regarded as a rhetorical device, intended to suggest that the writer is reasoning carefully, rather than as a sign that he is thinking logically. Some forms of thought which are related to formal logic, however, do function usefully in the structuring of sequences of genuine thought. Two of the most frequently employed modes of quasi-logical thought are experimentation and generalization.

The pattern of experimentation involves a question and a sequence of response leading to the acceptance of one hypothesis as the answer or thesis. Thus we might raise the question, "How did Tarzan die?" and propose answers such as "He had a heart attack" until we found one that seemed to fit best with the evidence. This kind of experimental pattern is, of course, an imitation of experiments conducted outside language, like experiments in scientific laboratories. In such experimental discourse the solution to one question often leads to the formulation of another:

Q. How did Tarzan die?
A. He was poisoned.
Q. Who did it?

A detective story is an imitation of the experimental method. In a sequence of the experimental kind, we may find that certain sub-questions have to be dealt with in order to clarify aspects of the larger question, and certain sub-theses have to be asserted before the general thesis can be reached:

Why would anybody want to poison Tarzan?
Maybe somebody wanted him out of the way.
Why would anybody want him out of the way?
Maybe they hated his guts.
But everybody loves Tarzan.
Everybody?
Name somebody who doesn't.
Cheetah?
Don't be ridiculous.
Then who . . . ?

We have presented this sequence in the form of a dialogue, but the questions and answers in discourse are usually thought of as belonging to one mind that is ordering a sequence of thought. The basic pattern of beginning with a question, testing possible answers, and concluding with the one right answer, is used over and over again in writing. A related sequence is the sequence of generalization.

The sequence of generalization tends to assume that a question has been asked which it then proceeds to answer. Actually, this kind of sequence comes in more than one form. One is simply the form of experimentation without the questions. Its structure is basically this: Because A is true, and B is true, and C is true, D (which follows from them) must be true also. Or this: A, B, and C are true; therefore D (which follows from them) is true. The because-therefore sequence is the fundamental form of generalization. Another form is simply a reversal of the because-therefore order, in which the conclusion is presented first: D is true because A, B, and C are true. This pattern, which we can call the statement-evidence form, makes an assertion and then explains it so that the reader knows the conclusion *before* he sees the evidence and can be alert for missing links in the chain of causes or for unwarranted assumptions or unreasonable connections. The form which ends with "therefore" has more of a narrative dimension (like the detective story), which may make it more interesting to read but less easy to test analytically.

These forms seldom operate with a simple structure of one conclusion or statement accompanied by a clearly connected chain of evidence. They depend on certain kinds of sub-structure, like these:

1. If A, then B; A is, so B must be.
2. If A then B; but no A, so no B.
3. If A then either B, C, or D; A, but no B or C; therefore D.
4. If A, then at least two of B, C, and D; A and B, but no C; therefore D.

And so on. These can get very complicated, and they can be heightened rhetorically in various ways. For instance, when the inevitable "therefore" is reached, instead of merely stating it, the writer can ask a question, like "What then?" Because the writer has worked things so that the answer is inescapable, this kind of question is called rhetorical. It is not so much a question as a way of provoking the reader to supply the inevitable answer.

The forms we have been considering here are related to the syllogistic formulae of logic (see page 60) but they are used more often in written thought. The important thing about written thought, however, as distinguished from purely logical thought, is that its most crucial aspect is definition. Definition is so crucial to written thought that it requires a section of its own—certainly the most important section in this chapter.

Definition

We are defining all the time. Every name, every noun, is a definition. No objects, nor actions, nor qualities exist in language—only names for objects (nouns) and names for actions (verbs) and names for qualities (modifiers—adjectives and adverbs). Writing involves getting the best fit possible between our definitions and the things they define. Much of our thought in writing is just an attempt to define more accurately the things we are talking about. And as soon as we make the attempt to define we stop merely naming and start a process of sequential thought. Consider the following syllogism:

All A's are B's
C is an A
Therefore: C is a B.

Now turn it into writing, like this:

All chimpanzees are fools
Cheetah is a chimpanzee.
Therefore: Cheetah is a fool.

The first sentence (major premise) defines chimpanzees as fools. But what does this mean? In what sense might a chimpanzee be a fool? What *is* a fool. The second sentence (minor premise) defines Cheetah as a chimpanzee. In both sentences the first noun is said to belong to a class or category which is defined by the second noun. But these nouns do not all exist on the same level. "Cheetah" defines a class of one: it is a proper name, a perfect definition, like "Tarzan." Chimpanzee defines a species of animal which can be described in considerable biological detail with scientific precision. But "fool" points to a class with no boundaries. "Fool" really defines the attitude of the person defining rather than a group of things that exist independently of him. We can determine accurately whether or not Cheetah belongs to the class of chimpanzees, but we have no foolproof test for a fool.

When we really think in writing we elaborate the process of definition. In this process we use two faculties which John Locke and the men of his time defined as "wit" and "judgment." In Locke's definition, "wit" is the faculty that sees resemblances between things; judgment is the faculty that discriminates. These two mental "faculties" are really aspects of a larger definition of the mind, and in particular they define that part of the mind that makes definitions. This whole vision of the mind is a fiction, of course, like all visions of the mind. When we speak of the human brain, we speak of something which has material existence and can be weighed and measured. But when we speak of mind—as opposed to brain—we are giving a name to an aspect of human behavior. When we use words like "mind" or "soul" we are making an assertion about human nature, an assertion based on a definition.

Just as the concept of mind itself is a useful fiction, and perhaps a "true" one, Locke's division of the mind into parts is also both fictional and useful. Even though "wit" and "judgment" do not exist in the same way that chimpanzees and brains do, they have their own kind of reality in the world of existence. Locke, of course, simply constructed a mental model of the mind and assigned names to two "faculties" which he then held responsible for two distinguishable aspects of mental process. Constructing models of this sort is one important way of defining. Models enable us to "see" and comprehend things we might otherwise miss. But it is important to remember that they are only simplified versions of complicated things; that they may obscure important aspects of the reality they represent as well as bring other aspects into a brighter light.

The making of models as a form of definition is closely related to the process of making metaphors. We sometimes think of metaphor as a poetic device, but it is actually a fundamental linguistic process. It is an aspect of naming. Every time we talk of one thing in terms of another thing we are using metaphor. In the last paragraph the words "obscure" and "brighter light" use a notion of the way light and darkness operate in the world of the senses to talk about an operation which is purely mental. This is metaphor operating in a very small way. In reading, we might not even notice the metaphor in the word "obscure," which means literally "to darken." The metaphor in "brighter light" is more obvious, but we are still quite likely to take it in its metaphoric sense without being aware of the literal sense behind the metaphor.

We are not holding this metaphor up as a brilliant example of metaphor-making, but as a typical one—the kind most writers make all the time. Excellence in writing depends to a great extent on the writer's awareness of the metaphors he uses. The aware writer can carry his metaphors just to the point where they illuminate the most for him and drop them whenever they begin to hinder his vision more than they help it.

Two of the most important aspects of the metaphorical process are extension and mixing. We extend a metaphor by continuing to talk about one thing in terms of another. Like this:

> A nation is a lot like a human being. The intellectuals are a nation's brain. Soldiers and police are its fists. The mailmen are its nervous system, transportation workers circulate its life-blood. Working people are the heart and lungs of a nation. Businessmen are the stomach. What would happen to a body if its parts no longer worked together? What will happen to us if we cease to work together?

A metaphor extended in this way becomes an analogy. Such analogies are a crucial part of all persuasive writing. In public affairs, historical analogies like the following are used all the time:

> The situation *now* is like the situation *then. Then* they did X, and Y was the result. If we do X *now*, Y will happen again. Is this what we want?

Historical analogies are dangerous because they do not *seem* to be metaphorical. But no two situations in life are ever exactly alike. Therefore, every time we make a historical analogy we are making a metaphor, using our wit. Any metaphor used as an analogy in a process of argument had better be subjected to judgment as well as wit. The tendency of analogies is to oversimplify unless they are qualified. Whenever someone says, "Situation A is like situation B"—watch out! If he says situation A is like situation B with respect to X, Y, and Z but different with respect to P, Q, and R—watch out anyway, but give the fellow a chance; he is inviting you to think with him. And in your own writing, try to invite your reader to think with you by using analogies with care.

For instance, the nation-body analogy developed above, and all the little analogies developed by extension of the big one, is in serious need of qualification. Why should businessmen be the stomach? Why not the consumers? Maybe businessmen should be the heart. Maybe politicians should. Maybe intellectuals are not really the whole brain but just one of its lobes. A lot depends on your point of view. Maybe the whole analogy oversimplifies too much and should be discarded entirely. Still, it provides a stimulus to thought, a place to begin. Any writer using such an analogy will have to decide finally whether it does more good than harm to his writing, and he will have to use it so as to maximize the good and minimize the harm.

Another variation of metaphorical thinking involves mixing metaphors. Many textbooks condemn all mixed metaphors, but actually, as with most other things, the mixing of metaphors has good features as well as bad ones. Two or more different metaphors put together may work as a check on one another, preventing any single metaphor from turning into an oversimplified analogy. If we suggest that A is like B in one respect, but like C in another, and D in yet a third, we will prevent anyone from assuming that A and D are identical. A political columnist once raised the question of whether our government was like the poet's "wonderful one-horse shay" which ran perfectly for a hundred years and then went entirely to pieces, or like Everett Dirkson's vision of the government as a "scow" that was slow and clumsy but unsinkable. These two metaphors which relate the government to vehicles of transportation, as the columnist combined them, provide a useful pattern for thought. The two images are not confused; they are brought together purposefully and deliberately. This is quite different from the mixing of metaphors that often develops when a writer thoughtlessly combines conflicting images. The combination of clichés, in particular, often leads to a ludicrous mixing of metaphors. This sort of writing is a sure sign that the writer is not thinking:

Unless the ship of state is steered more carefully, we will get off the track and end up in the blind alley of revolution.

Ship, track, alley? Three vehicular clichés strung together make a mixture of metaphor quite different from the columnist's scow and shay.

When metaphor is being used properly, it is an aspect of the process of comparison and contrast which is the foundation of our thought. By perceiving similarities with our wit and differences with our judgment, we take proper mental possession of the world we inhabit. The formal classroom exercise of writing papers that call for the comparing and contrasting of two things has its basis in the recognition that this process of comparing and contrasting is vital to our thinking. The important thing to remember is that comparison and contrast need one another. In written thought, one of them without the other is usually irresponsible. Categories need internal distinctions; analogies need limits and exceptions. Wit comes first; it is the creative faculty. But judgment, the critical faculty, completes it and makes it whole.

DEBATE AND DIALECTIC

A thought process related to comparison and contrast is that in which a thesis and a counter-thesis or antithesis are brought together. This process tends to take either of two forms. In the form of debate, the counterargument (or counterarguments—there may be more than one) is brought forward by the writer in order to be disposed of. He is really trying to anticipate the argument of someone whose thoughts on the matter at hand are opposed to his own, so that he can disarm that opponent in advance. Sometimes the writer will dishonestly present in his work a representative of the opposed views as a "straw man" that can easily be blown aside. The more thoughtful and imaginative the writer is, however, in presenting the views opposed to his own, the more properly persuasive his piece is likely to be. When this creation of opposed views takes the form of a balance, the form has become dialectical, so that thesis and antithesis must be resolved not by upholding either one of them but by combining both into a new synthesis. This form is a kind of enactment of a thought process leading to a conclusion rather than an argument which presents the conclusions of a process already complete. Debate is related to that form of oral argument in which two teams take opposite sides, each arguing for victory. Dialectic is a form of discussion in which compromise rather than victory is taken to be the end of the process. Debate is a performance by a closed mind. Dialectic is the struggle of an open mind.

OUTLINES AND SUMMARIES

The end of this chapter on sequences of thought in writing seems the appropriate place for a word on outlines. It used to be customary to teach students in writing classes how to make a standard kind of outline. Thus the student learned the three-part division of a theme (introduction, body, and conclusion), or the outline by topics and subtopics:

I. Tarzan
    A. Eating habits
        1. liquids
           a. soup, plain
           b. soup, poisoned
        2. solids
           a. . . .
           b. . . .
    B. Working habits . . .
    C. Playing Habits . . .

II. Cheetah . . .

        etc. . . . to

XII. Conclusion.

As you may have guessed, we are skeptical of the value of outlines beyond a sketchy list of a possible order of topics. This attitude of ours is related to our belief that *writing is not something which follows thinking, but is itself a way of thinking.* If you have a complete and perfect outline of something that you have not yet written, chances are you have not thought about it creatively and will not. Some plan is probably essential to writing. Sometimes a mental plan is sufficient. Other times a written plan will be useful. But it ought to be loose and open enough to allow for drastic alteration in the course of composition. Writing should be a voyage of discovery, not a guided tour.

A finished piece of writing, on the other hand, should be clear enough in its order that a good outline could be abstracted from it, or an intelligible summary made of it. An outline or summary can be a very useful part of proofreading and perfecting a supposedly finished piece of work, because it may reveal that the work is not finished after all.

M7

These materials may prove appropriate for group discussion or for individual assignments in writing—or both.

Take the following items of raw information:

1. Toadstools are poisonous.
2. Frank is dead.
3. Ernest gave Frank a toadstool.

a. Using the information above as a point of departure, construct some syllogisms, both valid and invalid, true and untrue, about Frank, Ernest, poison, toadstools, and death.

b. Using the same basic materials, and confining yourself to simple sentences, write a narrative of about fifty words.

c. Rewrite your narrative for maximum emotional effect. Keep it under one hundred words if you can.

M8

a. Write a brief description of a place known to the members of your group. Present your description in three forms:

1. precise but unemotional,

2. so as to make the place attractive,

3. so as to make the place unattractive.

b. Discuss the problems and solutions of all three forms of description. Are the solutions mainly matters of sequence, of structure, or of individual words?

M9

a. Write a brief paragraph about something you like, in which you discuss it in terms of a single, consistently developed metaphor.

b. Write another paragraph about the same thing, but this time discuss it in terms of as many different metaphors as you can bring together in a short paragraph.

c. Write a third paragraph in which you discuss the thing you like without using a single metaphor.

d. Discuss the problems and solutions you found in writing each paragraph.

M10

Select a controversial topic and write about it in each of the following ways:

a. Two paragraphs: In the first, present one side of the controversy. In the second, refute every point you made in the first, and state your conclusion.

b. Three paragraphs: In the first present one side; in the second, an opposed side; in the third, a compromise.

c. Discuss the problems and solutions members of your group found in dealing with the controversy in each of these ways. Have some controversies seemed more appropriately treated in one or the other manner?

PART TWO
CONTEXTS OF WRITING

The Existence of a Written Work

A written work exists, first of all, because someone has written it. This statement may seem laughably simple, but it opens the way to seeing some less obvious aspects of the existence of a piece of writing. A written work also exists in order to be read by someone. The work is a kind of bridge connecting writer and reader. It establishes some sort of relationship between two individuals. This is important. Even a document like the Declaration of Independence, which bears many signatures, was at some point drafted by a single man, dipping his pen into an inkwell, mentally putting together subjects and predicates, scratching his thoughts on paper, crossing out, revising, reading over his own sentences with annoyance or satisfaction. And those words, made permanent and unalterable by printing and publication, still exist to be read by any other individual, at his own pace, with his own level of understanding, reacting with his own thoughts and feelings.

A written work communicates in a different way than a film, or a speech, or a program on radio or television communicates to us. Even if thousands of people read it, each act of reading is unique and individual. The reader is free to stop, go back, check up on things, or give up reading at any point. He has a freedom which hardly any other form of communication allows him. The writer has put his thoughts in permanent form, to be studied, appreciated, modified, or rejected by a reader who has time to react fully to those thoughts, examining them as carefully as he wants to. It is harder to fool people in writing than in those media which pass quickly before our senses and then vanish. When we are suspicious, we often find ourselves saying, "Put it in writing, will you?"

When a political figure, for instance, makes a speech to us on television, his image is present to all of us, but our images are not present to him. He sets the pace of thought and we must move at that pace or be lost. We can never say, "Hey, wait a minute, I don't believe that." And even if in our frustration we say it, we cannot make his words hold still for further examination. Marshall McLuhan has called TV a "cool" medium and writing a "hot" one, but only writing allows us time to reflect coolly on what has been said and respond coolly with a collected intelligence.

Writing is actually cool in another sense, as well, because reader and writer never confront one another directly. (If you write a note, hand it to someone, and watch him read it, this would be pretty direct contact, though less direct than talking face to face—but this is obviously a very special case. Normally the reader is not present at the writing of a work and the writer is not present at the reading.) This distance between writer and reader makes for special problems in the relationship between them. Let us consider these problems first from the writer's point of view.

To begin with, the writer must create for himself some image of the reader. If he is writing a letter to an intimate friend or relative, this act of imagination is probably unconscious and automatic. There is only one reader to consider, and this reader is very well known to the writer. But suppose Tarzan is writing a letter to Jane, and Jane lives in an apartment with some snoopy roommates. Suppose also that Jane is just a bit careless about leaving things around. This gives Tarzan a problem. He has to imagine more than one possible reader: his beloved Jane by herself or a gaggle of other girls giggling over his deepest feelings. He may well find this second possible readership so threatening as to prevent his writing a good letter to Jane at all.

The writer of a public document, such as a letter to the editor of a newspaper, has a different but related problem. He doesn't have to achieve an intimate prose style, but he does have to find some way of communicating effectively to whatever segment of the paper's readership he hopes to reach. Of course, a lot of writers of letters to the editor don't really want to communicate; they just want to express themselves. They want to get something off their chests and don't care whether they enlighten anybody or not. In effect, such a writer unconsciously imagines himself as his only reader; he dutifully reads his letter with great appreciation when it graces the paper's editorial page. As a general rule someone who chooses to express himself rather than communicate with another person is as much of a bore in writing as he is in speaking. Even a diary, to be worth anything, must be written with the writer's future self in mind as a reader, and the better the diarist is at predicting the interests of that future self, the more rewarding the diary will prove to be.

So, effective communication in writing depends in part on the writer's ability to imagine his reader. But this is only one aspect of his work. He must also provide in the written work itself a role for that reader to play. In writing a letter to the editor, you may imagine a kind of composite reader of a sort appropriate to a particular paper (obviously the

Wall Street Journal and the communist *Daily Worker* do
not have the same readership) but then you must also
imagine some particular role which that reader is capable
of assuming. You may appeal to his better nature by en-
couraging him to adopt the role of public-spirited citizen;
or you may play on the poor fellow's weaknesses by putting him in the position of an over-taxed, downtrodden,
victim of his government. There are, of course, dozens of
possible roles that a writer can encourage his reader to
adopt: student, friend, jury, wise man, bigot, and so on.
Presumably any particular piece of writing will encourage
one dominant role for the reader of that work, but the role
may be a blend of several qualities. One of the great tests
of a writer's *skill* is his ability to get readers to accept the
roles he has imagined for them. And one of the great tests
of a writer's *value* is his ability to get real readers to accept
roles that require an expansion of thought and feeling from
them rather than a retreat into stock response and prejudice.

The reader, of course, is not the only person whose role
is implied in a written work. The writer, too, has a role
implied in the work, and a reciprocal relationship must
exist between his role and the reader's. If the writer wants
to play teacher, he must get the reader to play student. If
he wants to play expert, he must get the reader to play
layman. If he wants to play friend of the reader, he must
get the reader to feel friendly toward him. Broadly speaking, there are three kinds of relationship the actual writer
can try to establish between himself-in-the-work and the
reader-implied-by-the-work. He can write *down* to the
reader: "As an expert on ecology I assure you that Tarzan
has upset the balance of jungle life." He can write *up* to the
reader: "I'm just an ignorant country ape myself, but

maybe educated folks like you can tell me if that Tarzan feller ain't messin' up our jungle." Or he can write level with the reader: "You and I have had enough experience of the jungle to understand this Tarzan situation."

Most private writing (letters, diaries, and the like) establishes a level relationship between writer and reader. Most public writing is written down, from the man who knows to those who want to know. Our political rhetoric seems to require a combination of down and up, so that we often find our leaders addressing us in this manner:

Fellow apes! I, Tarzan, your elected leader, agree to accept the heavy burden of responsibility that you have thrust upon me despite my unworthiness. And I want you to know that Jane and Cheetah and all of us—a simple family—will work night and day, humbly, to give you the kind of government you deserve.

Thus far we have been considering the existence of a written work mainly in terms of the writer-reader relationship which every work must seek to establish. And we have concentrated on this problem from the writer's point of view. Later in this chapter we will return to reconsider this relationship from the reader's point of view. But before reaching that point we must pause to examine another relationship which is vital to the existence of a written work. In most such works (except for highly personal forms like the love letter and some kinds of imaginative literature) the writer-reader relationship is only a means to the end of effective communication. And effective communication involves a "message" sent by the writer and received by the reader. A written work is simply one kind of message. But what is a message? How does it exist?

A message is something that involves a special relationship between a language and the world. It has been said that a language is something like a map of the world. It is a way of organizing the world's features so that they can be understood. But no two languages "map" the world in exactly same way. One of the good reasons for studying a second language is to see how different the world looks on the map of another language. A really good look at another language may even teach us to see the world differently. But all messages must be framed in one language or another. Simple messages ("No Smoking") can be translated without loss from one language to another ("Défense de Fumer"). More complex ones change more in the translation.

Just as language is a sort of map of the world, a message is a large-scale map of a small part of the world. The writer of a message cannot say anything about the world that his language will not let him say. Every new idea requires either new words or new combinations of old ones in order to take shape in language. Neither the world itself, nor any living language, will stand still. To make a new message is far harder than to repeat old ones. And in time, metaphors that once had life, and expressions that once were packed with thought, become dull and meaningless—tired clichés. To make a message that is new—and meaningful—that is a problem which tests the linguistic resources of the writer. The writer has his expertise, his sensitivity, his imagination, his honesty to offer in making his little map, his message. He need not make a great breakthrough in science or philosophy to write something worth our reading. A unique point of view, honestly presented, in adequate language—that is enough. To manage this much, of course, the writer must preserve his individuality. If he repeats clichés unthinkingly, he abandons his uniqueness and gives his being into the care of others.

Language is one of the battlegrounds—perhaps the most important—where we must fight to defend our freedom. Our linguistic freedom is threatened from a number of directions. Most of us are not at home in the whole of our language. We use habitually that part of the language which is used by others in our locale, our profession, our class. In extreme cases we may regularly use a dialect quite different from "standard English," or a professional jargon which is just as unintelligible to outsiders as a local dialect. Now certain ways of thinking are built into certain sublanguages. Slogans like "white supremacy" and "black power" exemplify whole sets of mind. The attitudes shape the vocabulary and the vocabulary solidifies the attitudes. Managers who are used to thinking about those working under them as "personnel" may be unable to perceive their "personnel" as people—human beings with individual needs and feelings.

The writer must find language that is appropriate to himself, to his subject, and to his reader: language he can handle adequately, which is capable of presenting the subject properly, and can be understood by the reader. And this same language must be used to generate a writer-reader relationship which will contribute to the effectiveness of the message itself. The temptations to sloppiness and dishonesty are great. And sometimes, with the best will in the world, a writer will simply find himself inadequate to part or all of the job required by a particular piece of writing. Still, the attempt is important if the problem being considered is important. Trying to get our thoughts in order is a way of discovering aspects of a problem we have not yet faced. Pages of writing communicated only to the waste basket may be of great value to the person who wrote them, even though they were fit for no other reader's eyes. This means that public figures whose speeches are ghost-written by experts at manipulating audiences, on the basis of memoranda submitted by other experts on particular problems, deprive themselves of a crucial exercise in thinking. The ghostwritten speech based on the expert's memorandum, delivered over television by a carefully made-up political figure, seems perfectly designed to produce a credibility gap; because the man who utters the words has not earned them, has not found them for himself while struggling to apply his language to a problem. This is, of course, two writing-instructors' views of a complex situation. How accurate it is, the reader must determine for himself. Which brings us to a consideration of the reader's situation with respect to the existence of a written work.

A written work offers its reader a role to play in relation to the role assumed by the writer of the work, and it offers him a message to understand and respond to—a map or view of some aspect of the world. The reader's problem is how to react to both the message delivered and the role assigned. He must be fair but critical. He must be aware of the way all writers create roles for readers and aware of the way language shapes and limits all written thought. If the reader is totally uncritical, accepting everything, he abandons too much of himself and loses his individuality. But if he is totally suspicious, rejecting everything, he cuts off his own possibilities for growth and change. Clearly, reading requires a balance of acceptance and criticism. The reader must try out the role offered him and test the message presented to him. He must allow part of himself to go into the work, accepting its language, seeing the world as the writer intended him to. And the further from his own point of view the role offered him is, the harder it will be for him to accept it. At the same time, a part of the reader must be standing off, watching himself in the role which the work has required him to accept. This critical part of the reader must ask whether that role suits him, is good for him, expends or contracts his being. To accept the role of student is demeaning unless the teacher is worthy of the student. To be flattered, on the other hand, and have one's own prejudices reinforced, though very comforting, can be even more demeaning. The devil is a rhetorician, and his principle weapon is flattery.

Even more important for a reader than scrutinizing the role he accepts is scrutinizing the message he receives. First of all, of course, he must actually receive it. He must try to understand it as it seems to be intended. Then, he must measure the accuracy of this map against his own vision of the world. In particular, he must ask whether the language of the work is adequate to the subject of it. Are the names given to things sufficiently accurate in describing the things? Do the relations among these names bring some situation into clearer focus, or do they hide, obscure, or slide over important aspects of the subject. How, for instance, do the following sentences differ in describing the clash between Jane and Tarzan that we have been working with? Watch the italicized words and phrases in particular.

a. Tarzan and Jane had a *little marital spat.*
b. Jane led a *demonstration for women's rights* against Tarzan.
c. Tarzan *pacified* Jane.
d. Tarzan *taught* Jane *a lesson.*
e. Tarzan *educated* Jane.
f. Tarzan *violated* Jane's *civil rights.*

g.   Jane started a *riot*.

h.   Jane *confronted* Tarzan.

" 'What is truth?' said jesting Pilate, and would not stay for an answer." Thus Bacon condemned the administrator who signed Jesus Christ's death warrant. But Pontius Pilate was no joker. Like many another administrator he finally decided that truth is what the majority say it is. He took a vote. Jesus lost. Did he deserve to? Was Jesus a long-haired, trouble-making fanatic? Was He the son of God? The king of the Jews? A nice Jewish boy who was led astray by a bunch of drunken fishermen? All of the above? None of the above?

One thing is certain, the names things are given are immensely important, and so are the definitions we give those names. The reader must ask himself continually how the names in what he reads relate to the things he is reading about. He must begin by hoping the writer was honest, careful, sensitive, and intelligent. But he must be quite ready to be disappointed all along the line. And the writer —where does this leave him? Why, he must obviously pretend to be honest, careful, sensitive, and intelligent. Pretend? Yes. Writing is an art. *We* think (like all right-thinking people and especially you, reader) that a writer should try to *be* these things, to have these virtues. It is also important that he *seem* honest, careful, sensitive, and intelligent. He must be honest *in the work*, careful *in the work*, sensitive and intelligent *in the work*—and these qualities must make themselves felt *in the work*. Can a man *pretend* to have such qualities if he does not have them? None of us has them all the time. Pretending to have them is the way we develop them. Writing, done well, is a spiritual exercise as well as an intellectual one.

M11

At this point it will be useful to look at a variety of written works: newspapers, magazines, books. As a point of departure, we are quoting four passages from different writers. All of them are modern. Three are men. We will not supply the names of the writers, so as not to prejudice the group's speculations. Consider the following questions in relation to each passage:

1. What sort of writer-reader relationship does the passage imply? How is the writer characterizing himself (or herself)? What role is assigned to the reader?

2. Consider the relationship between the language of each passage and the world. What part or aspect of the world is being presented through these words? What linguistic resources are being employed? How adequate is the language to the ideas?

3. Which passage is most interesting? Which is truest? To what extent is your judgment a result of the rhetoric of the passage (writer-reader relationship) and to what extent is it a result of the perception presented (language-world relationship)?

4. Which passage was written by a woman? Evidence?

5. Consider the use of metaphor in these passages. Which is most metaphorical? Which least? Which uses metaphor most effectively?

6. Which passage is most abstract? Are the abstractions effective?

A. A lead-pencil has a point, an argument may have a point, remarks may be pointed, and a man who wants to borrow five pounds from you only comes to the point when he asks you for the fiver. Lots of things have points: especially weapons. But where is the point to life? Where is the point to love? Where, if it comes to the point, is the point to a bunch of violets? There is no point. Life and love are life and love, a bunch of violets is a bunch of violets, and to drag in the idea of a point is to ruin everything. Live and let live, love and let love, flower and fade, and follow the natural curve, which flows on, pointless.

B.   We may distinguish both true and false needs. "False" are those which are superimposed upon the individual by particular social interests in his repression: the needs which perpetuate toil, aggressiveness, misery, and injustice. Their satisfaction might be most gratifying to the individual, but this happiness is not a condition which has to be maintained and protected if it serves to arrest the development of the ability (his own and others) to recognize the disease of the whole and grasp the chances of curing the disease. The result is then euphoria in happiness. Most of the prevailing needs to relax, to have fun, to behave and consume in accordance with the advertisements, to love and hate what others love and hate, belong to this category of false needs.

C.   Is it really so difficult to tell a good action from a bad one? I think one usually knows right away or a moment afterward, in a horrid flash of regret. And when one genuinely hesitates—or at least it is so in my case—it is never about anything of importance, but about perplexing trivial things, such as whether to have fish or meat for dinner, or whether to take the bus or subway to reach a certain destination, or whether to wear the beige or the green. The "great" decisions—those I can look back on pensively and say, "That was a turning point"—have been made without my awareness. Too late to do anything about it, I discover that I have chosen. And this is particularly striking when the choice has been political or historic. For me, in fact, the mark of the historic is the nonchalance with which it picks up an individual and deposits him in a trend, like a house playfully moved by a tornado. My own experience with Communism prompts me to relate it, just because it had this inadvertance that seems to me lacking in the true confessions of reformed Communists. Like Stendhal's hero, who took part in something confused and disarrayed and insignificant that he later learned was the battle of Waterloo, I joined the anti-Communist movement without meaning to and only found out afterward, through others, the meaning or "name" assigned to what I had done. This occurred in the late fall of 1936.

D. When I contemplate the accumulation of guilt and remorse which, like a garbage-can, I carry through life, and which is fed not only by the lightest actions but by the most harmless pleasures, I feel Man to be of all living things the most biologically incompetent and ill-organized. Why has he acquired a seventy-years' life span only to poison it incurably by the mere being of himself? Why has he thrown Conscience, like a dead rat, to putrefy in the well?

Kinds of Writing

There is no such thing as just plain writing. The business of producing a written work is so highly artificial that no one does it without giving some thought to the form he is using—which means giving some thought to the way others have used the form. In language we learn first by imitating before we can move on to generate our own particular varieties of linguistic form. It does not, for instance, come to us as an inspiration from on high that we should begin a letter by writing "Dear Tarzan" or some variation on this basic pattern. We *learn* to do this as we learn the other forms of linguistic behavior. Learning a form has one big advantage. It enables us to benefit from a good deal of trial and error which lies behind the development of the form Following the tried and true form we gain a facility and intelligibility which would be hard to achieve without it. But learning a form has one terrible disadvantage. The form has a tendency to become a limit, a groove that restricts our thought to established patterns. ("Tried and true"? Who said that? Are all the usual forms usual because they are true, or true because they are usual? When does the "tried" become "untrue"?) Just as our language gives us a limited map of an infinitely varied world, an established linguistic form gives us a narrowly selective view of a small piece of the linguistic map. There is no way around form, just as there is no way around language. We must go *through*, mastering language and form, to achieve our own written version.

Most of the written forms available to us are designed to suit particular subjects and to reach particular audiences. A form implies a certain kind of relationship between writer and reader, and a certain kind of message. Some forms are very personal and natural, like the diary or the letter to a close friend. In these forms, writer and reader share an interest in one another, and often share a highly personal idiom. The diarist, of course, is the extreme case of identification of interest between writer and reader, and some diarists have written to themselves in "secret" languages or special versions of shorthand which no other reader was supposed to find intelligible. At the opposite extreme are certain kinds of public documents, including newspaper stories, government press releases, advertising copy, letters to the editor, popular books, and so on. Between these two extremes we have all sorts of writing designed for audiences limited in one way or another. Certain publications aim at narrowly specialist audiences, like doctors, or English teachers, or motorcyclists, or bird-watchers. In a way, the narrower the audience becomes, the easier it is to find appropriate forms for addressing it. Whenever a person becomes a member of a special group he begins to pick up the forms appropriate to the group—not just written forms but a whole pattern of behavior. This means that he can easily find an appropriate writer-reader relationship with the other members of that group, and he can easily determine when he has something to say about the subject of the group's common interest which the other members will want to hear.

Thus far, we have sketched a kind of continuum of possible writing situations, for which appropriate forms are likely to present themselves. The continuum ranges from private and personal at one end to public and general at the other. And in between come the various kinds of limited writing for special audiences. Sorts of writing which are circulated privately among members of a group, like business or government memoranda, or the "house" papers or magazines of clubs or corporations, belong on one end of the continuum. Things which are published but aim at special groups, like boating magazines or medical journals, belong more to the center. Newspapers with the highest circulation and most general kind of interest are at the other end, the public end; diaries, of course, are the most private of all.

Now, what is the situation of student writing with respect to all this? As a *person* who happens at the moment to be in a writing class, he (or she) probably writes some letters to friends and other essentially private things. As a *citizen* of a community (school or town) he may write letters to the editor or something of that nature. Ultimately, as a professional, he will probably do some more or less technical writing in connection with his work: applications, letters, reports, memoranda, studies, articles, suggestions, and so on. But as a *student*, what kind of writing will he do? And how will his writing as a student relate to the whole continuum of writing possibilities?

There is something very strange about the position of a student of writing, which needs to be examined. First of all, the student has to write whether he wants to or not—whether he has anything to say or not—and whether there is anyone he wants to say it to or not. He is not really on the continuum of normal writing possibilities at all. He can be assigned the task of writing something personal ("My Jungle Summer with Tarzan and Jane"), or something public (a letter to the editor of the *Jungle Gazette* about the harsh treatment of migrant apes on Tarzan's plantation), or something technical (a research paper on jungle ecology). But such assignments are highly artificial (a) because they are assigned, (b) because their real reader (the teacher) is not the reader for whom the form is ostensibly designed, and (c) bcause their real purpose (improvement in writing) is not their ostensible purpose.

The problem, then, for the student and the teacher of writing, is to find some way to deal with the highly artificial situation of writing in a writing class. It should be obvious that this problem is more acute than the problem of writing for a history class or an art class or any other class which a student has *elected* because he is genuinely interested in the subject matter. In such cases he is becoming a member of a limited-interest group, and should be able to adjust to the forms of writing which are current among the group. The question is how to turn a writing class into an interest group.

The solution can be approached in two quite different ways. We have heard of one very successful attempt, which solved the problem not by turning the class into an interest group but by putting each student in a person-to-person relationship with the teacher. In this class each student wrote letters to the teacher, which he answered. This method, of course, keeps the teacher very busy, writing to each student in the class, but if the teacher is not so burdened as to make this impossible, it is one of the most natural and effective means ever devised for taking the artificiality out of writing for a class. The students' letters bear some resemblance to "themes" or "papers," and the teacher's letters perform some of the functions of "corrections" on student themes. The letters can be "about" whatever subject the class would normally be considering. But this way the student can write more naturally and freely to begin with, and he can learn something about how to treat the subject by comparing the teacher's messages with his own. The student can learn by reading and writing as naturally as he learned to talk by listening and speaking.

Another way to solve the problem of writer-reader relationship in courses takes the opposite tack. Instead of establishing a personal "letter" relationship between each student and the teacher, a general interest group is established among the whole class. Using this procedure, every student in writing assumes that what he writes is written for all the others—including the instructor, of course. Every written work need not be seen by every member of the class, but works judged interesting by the instructor or by a screening committee of students should be made available to the whole group in some way (xerox, projection, reading aloud, etc.). It is important to establish an actual audience for the writer to contemplate. Writing for a whole class sometimes eliminates certain kinds of unreal verbiage which students mistakenly assume their teachers require of them. (The letter system should achieve the elimination of the unauthentic in its own way, too.) This readership of classmates can then be turned into a limited interest group in either of two ways. One way is to find a subject that actually engages the interest of the whole group and use that as the focus of student writing. Another way is for the group to *pretend*, knowingly and deliberately, to be something it isn't, and to direct student writing at this imaginary group. A class can adopt the role of any sort of recognizable group: feminists, vegetarians, English teachers, Democrats, Republicans, radicals, conservatives. Anything within the group's imaginative and intellectual grasp can be established as the imaginary focus of interest. Similarly, the writers can adopt imaginary relationships to the group while trying to persuade it to take plausible but imaginary courses of action.

The same class, of course, can find a genuine center of interest in some common subject. It is very important, we believe, for a group of writing students either to find a genuine center of interest or to be clearly aware that they are adopting an imaginary kind of limited interest for a specific purpose. One of the principal causes of bad student writing has to do with this aspect of the writer's psychology. If a student writer finds himself preparing an "assignment" on a subject that does not concern him, for an audience of one, his teacher, who seems to be very different from him in many ways, including his inexplicable devotion to this dull subject—we have a situation which will inevitably produce bad writing—which is of course bad reading for the teacher. Often the student in such a situation will try to fake a genuine interest in this subject, or he will try to guess what the teacher wants said and say just that. The resulting phoniness of mental process leads to the generation of feeble sentences, carelessly written and casually proofread—if the writer can bear to face what he has done in order to proofread it at all. This kind of debilitating hypocrisy is totally different from the temporary acceptance of an imaginary attitude agreed upon by student and teacher to begin with. A fiction is not a lie, because it involves no attempt to deceive. But the hypocritical pretense of interest where there is no interest is a very damaging kind of deceit—damaging to the writer-reader relationship, and finally most damaging to the writer himself, who may begin to believe his own deception and build his life on a false position.

Thus, trying to find a center of genuine interest for a writing class is more dangerous than adopting provisionally an imaginary one. But if a genuine center of interest can be found, it provides opportunities for serious and straightforward thought that no imaginary interest can quite supply. The most frequently and successfully used center of interest for writing students is writing itself. A written work which truly captures the interest of students and teachers provides a fixed text which must be treated without falsification, and a rich complex of ideas and attitudes which will support serious and sensitive study. A written text often allows, even stimulates, highly personal and emotional reactions, but it also sits quietly waiting for the appropriateness of those reactions to be measured against the words that caused them. We can study written structures in highly abstract, unemotional ways, and we can test the values presented in written works against our own sense of values.

Actually, one can write "about" writing in at least four distinguishable ways, and since these ways also serve as the usual approaches to writing about other things, it may be useful to discuss each of them here. The basic approaches one can take to a written work or a situation in life are these four: *creative, personal, critical,* and *scholarly.* The four actually describe points on a continuum of possible approaches from the most immediate to the most detached. In a creative written response to a situation in life, one tries to imitate the situation, to merge with it, to get inside it, to reproduce it in some way. In a personal response, one concentrates on the way the situation affects the writer himself: what does *he* think of it, how does *he* feel about it? A critical response is a more detached effort to understand the situation and evaluate it (favorably or unfavorably) by comparing and contrasting it with other related situations. To be critical, the writer must be some-what detached in order to have perspective on the situation he is describing. A scholarly response to a situation involves research into its history, its causes, its processes, its effects. It may incorporate several critical views as well as other research data.

The same four approaches may be taken toward a written work. The creative response to a written work is to imitate or parody it, to get inside its form and re-create it in some way. The personal response is a report on the reader's reaction to the work, how it moved him, what he thinks about it. A critical response includes the personal but tries to objectify it by seeking in the work the causes of the response. Criticism tends toward the form of an evaluative argument or an interpretive argument—or a combination of the two. The reader tries to generalize from his personal response in order to maintain a thesis about the work, which will be convincing to others. A scholarly response will move further away from personal judgment and seek a broader context for the work, accounting for its nature and qualities as products of forces beyond it in the psychology of the author, or the society he lived in, or the nature of man.

The four kinds of approach we have been discussing here are not, of course, water-tight categories. There is always some measure of each one in all the others, and it is especially possible to combine any two that lie next to one another on the continuum of possibilities. Most writers are not equally gifted at all four kinds of writing, but all four should be encouraged in the study of writing, because they do exercise different aspects of the intelligence and the emotions.

M12

It is time for some extended work in writing on some appropriate subjects. The structural exercises in the next section will be more enjoyable and more useful if they are done alternately with larger and freer assignments. What assignments will be best? We cannot say. Individual teachers and students must determine this for themselves. And if they determine to just push right on and do the structural exercises, that will probably be all right too.

PART THREE

PRACTICE IN WRITING

All writing is practice in writing. But here we are concerned with practice in a very narrow sense: something like the finger exercises by Czerny that students of piano use to develop their muscular strength and co-ordination. The exercises we are going to provide here are of two kinds, analytic and synthetic; or seen in another way, critical and creative. In the pages that follow we will present some sentences and some longer sequences. In each case we will suggest some analytical procedures: ways of taking a sentence or sequence apart and studying its structures; and some synthetic procedures: ways of constructing new sentences and sequences related to the ones under examination. We feel strongly that for this book to be genuinely useful, both sorts of procedure must be practiced; just as we feel that the whole practical section of the book depends upon the theoretical section and seeks to realize concretely the value that resides in theoretical study.

The sentences we have selected for study are long sentences, for the most part, which test the writer's control and the reader's ability to follow. Our purpose in selecting long sentences is not to suggest that there is anything wrong with short ones. Obviousy all good writing in English requires variety of sentence structure and some alternation between long and short sentences. But for purposes of study and exercise the long sentence raises questions of coherence and development that the short sentence does not. Effective long sentences rely heavily on the repetitive element in parallel constructions for their coherence, and they develop by introducing new words into these constructions at crucial points. The long sentence is, of course, itself a sequence. Different writers may choose to deploy almost the same structure of words as a single sentence or a group of sentences, but the writer who chooses to suspend the period of his sentence rather than close it quickly must undertake to order that sentence with extra care so as to keep the reader with him. The sentences and sequences that follow here have all been constructed with that extra care. They are great sentences. Some of them are even famous—which is a fate few sentences achieve by themselves. They will repay study—analytic and synthetic—and will support prolonged examination.

For the first five of these sentences and sequences we have provided fairly elaborate commentary, often doing most of the analytic work ourselves. For the others we have provided only hints and questions, leaving the work to student and teacher.

S1

> Reading maketh a full man, conference a ready man, and
> writing an exact man.   SIR FRANCIS BACON

The most striking feature of S1 is its parallel structure. In the analysis of such constructions it is always useful to find some way to display this structure more fully—like this:

		1	2	3	4	5
S1a		Reading	maketh	a	full	man
S1b	and	conference		a	ready	man
S1c		writing		an	exact	man.

In this display we have taken care to arrange the three parallel clauses (S1a, S1b, and S1c) so that their repetitive structural elements fall into vertical columns. The five numbered columns can each be considered separately with an eye to its role in the structure of the sentence. In column 1 we find the same grammatical form (a noun made out of a verb) in all three clauses, but the words are different in each case. In column 2 we have the main verb of the sentence—the only verb in this case—in S1a, and a gap or ellipsis in S1b and S1c. In column 1 we find the use of the same grammatical *form*, making for coherence; along with three different lexical meanings (three different words, in this case), making for development. In column 2 we have an item which is strictly concerned with coherence—no developmental quality at all in itself. By leaving this item out of S1b and S1c, the writer has made his sentence more compact, relying on our ability to follow his parallel structure and supply the missing word where we need it.

Columns 3 and 5 are also strictly devoted to coherence. They are not developmental in themselves. But in column 4, as in column 1, we have the coherence of a repeated grammatical form (in this case an adjective) plus the development that is derived from the introduction of a new lexical item in each clause. Thus the main work of the sentence is being done by the words in columns 1 and 4. Let us examine them more closely. Returning to column 1, we can see that there is a continuity of meaning operating to link these words, as well as a grammatical continuity. All three words have to do with acts of language. But when we perceive that this category (act of language) includes all three words in column 1, we can also see that all three words are not on the same footing. Reading and writing are the opposite aspects of the same act. These words complement one another in a very close way. But what is the status of "conference" as a linguistic act? And why is it "conference" rather than "conferring" which would seem to fit the pattern even more neatly?

When we look closely at the word "conference" we can see that it actually includes *two* linguistic acts—talking and listening—which are the oral counterparts of writing and reading. This raises the question of why the writer of this sentence made that particular choice. He could obviously have added another clause, producing a sentence like this: "Reading maketh a full man, writing an exact man, talking a ready man, and listening a patient man." But he choose not to. Why? Here are some possibilities. First, his composition of this sentence may have been dominated by an apparently irrelevant habit of mind. The writer may simply have liked to think of things in groups of three, and thus, consciously or unconsciously, he may have made the necessary adjustments as he wrote. There is some evidence that this particular writer, Francis Bacon, did like triads and triplets, for he used them with great frequency. On the other hand, he may have felt that talking and listening are so closely related—much more so than reading and writing —that they properly belonged in a single category. It is possible, of course, that Bacon's final choice of sentence structure resulted from some interaction between these two processes: that his habitual method of constructing in threes combined here with his conception of these enumerated acts of language as being properly three rather than four. At any rate, the slightly different shape of the word "conference" may be designed to alert us to the fact that its status is also slightly different.

But what about the words in column 4? How do they contribute to the coherence and development of the sentence? Grammatically, of course, they are all adjectives which can properly modify the word "man." This gives them a certain coherence. But beyond that they all represent in this context desirable mental qualities. Fullness, here, signifies fullness of learning, fullness of ideas; readiness signifies a desirable alertness and quickness of understanding and response; and exactness signifies thoughtfulness and care in formulating ideas. The words in column 4 are coherent because they signify closely related qualities. They are developmental because each quality is distinct from the others. In a system of parallel development like this sentence, we can have either a pattern of random addition or of purposeful addition, which raises the question of whether S1a, S1b, and S1c could be rearranged in some other order without weakening the sentence in any way. Looked at in terms of our structural display of the sentence, this question invites us to consider the two sequences obtained by reading columns 1 and 4 vertically.

Is there any purposeful progression in the order reading-conference-writing? or in the order full-ready-exact? Reading is an act of reception; conference of give and take; writing of active projection. Similarly, fullness is a passive state, the result of reception; readiness is a passive state pointing strongly toward action; exactness is a quality demonstrable only in action. Thus, the examination of both columns indicates that the sentence is designed to move purposefully from the most passive and receptive actions and states to the most dynamic and projective. There is also an order of temporal arrangement and/or cause-and-effect arrangement working through the sentence, which implies that writing is the last action to be undertaken. After a person has read about a subject and conferred with others about it, then he shapes his own thoughts by the exacting process of written composition. Bacon's sentence, of course, exemplifies the process. It is a very careful, exact, piece of work.

S1 EXERCISES

ANALYTIC

We have already done a fairly thorough job of analysis on S1 and so will pose no further analytical questions here. But you might reconsider the above analysis in order to determine

    a.   what procedures used there you find especially useful or useless,

    b.   what parts of the analysis you find most convincing—and what least,

    c.   what aspects of the sentence the analysis has ignored.

SYNTHETIC

1.   Try the following ways of changing the meaning of the sentence while preserving its structure.

    a.   Find three new words for column 1, keeping the rest of the sentence as it is.

    b.   Find three new words for column 4 only.

    c.   Revise both columns 1 and 4 entirely, keeping the rest of the sentence.

2. Consider the effects of your changes. Have you produced nonsense? a serious new meaning? a parody of Bacon's meaning?

   a. Try deliberately to re-do exercises 1a, 1b, and 1c in two ways, one so as to generate new serious meanings and the other to create a parody of Bacon's meaning.

   b. Now consider the results of your revisions. In which case were you most successful at serious revision? In which case did you produce the best parody? Did others who did these exercises have the same experience? Do these results lead to any conclusion about the relationship of structure and meaning in this sentence? in general?

3. Now try to convey Bacon's meaning without using his sentence structure.

   a. Try it in one sentence.

   b. Try it in several.

   c. Try it keeping as many of his words as possible.

   d. Try it keeping as few of his words as possible.

   e. Consider the effectiveness of your various revisions.

   f. What conclusions about the relationship of structure and meaning can you derive from this exercise?

S2

   Histories make men wise, poets witty; the mathematics subtle, natural philosophy deep; moral grave, logic and rhetoric able to contend. SIR FRANCIS BACON

This is another sentence from further along in the same essay. Here Bacon is expanding the notion of fullness introduced in the earlier sentence, suggesting the different kinds of quality that men may develop by reading different kinds of books. Once again, parallel construction with its attendant ellipses is the dominant feature of the sentence. In the space below, complete a display of this sentence following the pattern we used for S1. (You must do this to follow the coming discussion.) Be sure to include the punctuation in column 4.

	1	2	3	4
S2a				
S2b				
S2c				
S2d				
S2e				
S2f				

As we see it, your display should have four columns and six horizontal lines as we indicate them above. Columns 2 and 3 reveal ellipses in every clause after S2a. Have you noticed one other small ellipsis in clause S2e, column 1? Column 1 yields us a list of varieties of reading, and column 4 a list of the different qualities that reading can develop. Looking at these two lists a number of features should strike us:

1. All the words in column 1 refer to subject matter except the second, "poets," which refers to the kind of writer rather than the kind of writing. Why?

2. All the qualities in column 4 are expressed in single words except the last. Why?

3. Each item in column 1 refers to a single kind of reading, except the last, which refers to two kinds. Why?

4. Though every clause is structurally identical, we have light punctuation at the end of S2a, S2c, and S2e; and heavy punctuation at the end of S2b, S2d, and S2f. Why?

The answers to some of these questions may be inter-related. Let us take the last one first. The punctuation, by its very arbitrariness, must reveal something about the author's intention in the whole sentence. But in order to get to this intention we must consider its effect. The punctuation takes a list of six items and turns it into a list of three double items. Why? Because Bacon likes to think of things in threes? Possibly. But there is more evidence bearing on this problem. In question 3 above we wondered why logic and rhetoric were put together in a single unit while all the other kinds of reading were given separate places. They *are* related, of course, since they are aspects of the formal study of language, and this may be the reason they have been brought together, just as talking and listening were brought together in S1 by the single word, "confer-ence." But that structural pressure to organize things in threes is operating here again. There seems to be more of rhetoric than of logic in this arrangement.

But what of the last item in column 4? Why is it not a single word? The reason may have to do with the rhythm of the sentence. "Able to contend" balances "logic and rhetoric" in a way, and it also falls into an iambic rhythm (dum-da-dum-da-dum) which gives a feeling of finality to the sentence. (In the first version of Bacon's essay this was the concluding sentence; later he extended the essay beyond this point.) But this consideration probably was not the primary one. The English language provides no single word for the concept Bacon wanted here. "Contentious," for instance, signifies a disposition to argue rather than the ability to do so. Its connotations are unfavorable and therefore inappropriate in this list of valuable qualities. "Eloquent" would imply a purely rhetorical kind of linguistic excellence, more concerned with moving an audience than with proving a case. The man who is "able to contend" in Bacon's view needs both logic and rhetoric to function effectively, because rhetoric without logic is empty and logic without rhetoric is dull. Thus S2f, which from one angle seemed the most arbitrary of the six clauses, from another seems the most complex and exact. But what are the other results of Bacon's division of his six clauses into three pairs?

If we look at column 4 with an eye to this pairing we see the following chain: wise-witty, subtle-deep, grave-able to contend. Wise and witty are linked in part because of their alliteration, and in part because they represent two quite different and somewhat opposed qualities. We can see a similar kind of opposition working through the other pairs, if we arrange them not in order of appearance but according to their meanings, in a new display:

1	2
wise	witty
deep	subtle
grave	able to contend

In this display the first column yields a list of words with common connotations of stability and reliability, while the second column yields connotations of flexibility and vigor. This balance of qualities suggests that the man who possesses them all will be astonishingly well rounded and balanced himself. And each column represents an element of coherence in the sentence, while each line read across— in either direction—is highly developmental.

If we turn our attention to the whole sentence as we originally displayed it to reveal its structure, and consider the column which lists the varieties of reading (column 1) as a system of three pairs, we do not discover such a neat system of oppositions as column 4 yielded. But we can see some principles of organization operating. Histories and poets are the most literary kinds of reading discussed here. The mathematics and natural philosophy (by which Bacon meant what we call natural science) are the most scientific. And moral philosophy, logic, and rhetoric are the most directly concerned with the citizen's behavior in the world —his actions and his words. Thus Bacon's system of thinking in pairs and triads can be seen as his way of ordering the world around him, making it manageable and communicable. This system oversimplifies but so do all systems and, in fact, all languages. Nowadays we prefer less rigid structures in the ordering of our sentences, but our best writers, flexible as their prose appears, often rely on fundamental structures much like Bacon's to shape their thought and strengthen their writing.

We have yet to examine the curious use of the word "poets" in S2b. Why "poets" instead of "poetry," which would be closer in form to "histories"? Why, in fact, "histories" instead of "history"? Here Bacon was up against the lexical and grammatical intractabilities of the English language, just as with the problem of finding a word for ability to contend in argument or debate. The statement "History makes men wise" in the English language would refer to events of history rather than books about it. But

Bacon wants to convey the idea that reading about history will produce wisdom. He also wants to suggest that reading many books on history is the best procedure. Thus he settles on "Histories make men wise," in which the plural noun "histories" serves both to prevent confusion between the events of history and books about it, and to suggest that many books rather than a few is what Bacon intends. He wishes next to turn to poetry and say something like "Poetry makes men witty." But here he runs into the reverse of the problem he had with history. We have no word in English for poetry books in the plural. We have "poetry" (always singular) and we have "poems"—but poems can be quite short, lacking the substance to balance "histories." And "poetry" will not go with "make"—being a singular noun, it requires an "s" on the verb: "poetry makes." In a parallel construction like this the verb (or any omitted word) is assumed to retain its original form in all the places where it is omitted by ellipsis. Thus "poets" is a solution, though not a perfect one, to the problem of filling the structure of the sentence. In S2c, "the mathematics" functions as a plural, so that it agrees with "make" (though we now use "mathematics" as a singular noun). But by the time he gets to S2d, Bacon gives up this attempt at grammatical consistency and uses a singular form, "philosophy," which is itself allowed to vanish in an ellipsis in S2e. "Logic and rhetoric," though each term is singular, make a plural subject together, ending the sentence on a harmonious grammatical note. But Bacon got away with something in S2d and S2e that a grammatical purist would find incorrect. For us, it is interesting to observe that he felt the strength of the grammatical need for a plural noun in S2b, but not in S2d. He seems to have felt that the grammatical pressure was eased

when he got far enough away from the verb. This shows
a shrewd sense of grammar, for in practice few readers
notice the inconsistency, which remains hidden until some
analysis like this one reveals it.

S2   EXERCISES

You have already (we trust) worked out the structural display of this sentence in lines and columns. And we have
again been fairly thorough in our analysis. Actually, this
sentence is so much like S1 that the same suggestions for
synthetic study that we made there may be followed here.
Only we are now in a position to ask one additional question. If you attempt the same synthetic procedures here
that you followed for S1, compare your results in both
cases to see if your work on S2 leads to the same conclusions about the relationship of structure and meaning, or
whether it suggests that some qualifications or modifica-
tions of your earlier conclusions are now necessary.

S3

> It hath been a question often disputed, but never de-
> termined, whether the qualities of the mind, or the com-
> position of the man, cause women most to like, or whether
> beauty or wit move men most to love.   JOHN LYLY

This is a more complicated affair than S1 or S2, and
therefore harder to diagram. In dealing analytically with
long, complex structures like this one, it is always useful
to abstract the basic structure of the sentence first. This
structure may be quite simple, but sometimes it is hidden
behind modifiers or interrupted by parenthetical elements,
so that the analyst must look carefully for such things as

the main verb and the conjunctions that govern the major sections of the sentence. In the case of S3 this basic structure is very simple indeed:

It hath been a question . . . whether . . . or . . . or whether . . . or . . . .

From this simple abstraction we can see that the main weight of the sentence is not in the main clause, and that the sentence is clearly structured by an elaborate set of parallels governed by the conjunctions "whether" and "or." When we make a structural display of the sentence, we get something like this:

		often disputed,	
S3a	It hath been a question	but	
		never determined,	

		1		2	3	4	5	6
		the qualities of the mind,						
S3b	whether	or	cause women most to like,					
		the composition of the man,						

		beauty	
S3c	or whether	or	move men most to love.
		wit	

(We have introduced numbered columns for clauses S3b and S3c only.)

Looking at this display, we should be struck by a number of features. Each clause contains one set of paired items, linked by "but" or "or." And each paired set, when viewed vertically, reveals an exact balance of word for word: often-never, qualities-composition, beauty-wit, and so on. And this balance frequently extends beyond the equating of word and word: there is an equality of syllables, even, in "often" and "never"; a quality which extends to alliteration in disputed-determined and mind-man. Our awareness of alliteration in these doubled structures should also alert us to the way that alliteration provides a coherence of sound pattern that extends though long stretches of the sentence: "question . . . qualities," "composition . . . cause," "whether . . . women . . . whether . . . wit," "mind . . . man . . . most . . . move . . . men most."

When we examine the vertical relationships between the parallel clauses S3b and S3c, we can see that despite the greater number of words in S3b, we have the identical structure in the two clauses. And beyond that, we have almost the identical meaning. The only really significant difference in meaning is the difference between "women" and "men" in column 3. Otherwise, that long phrase, "the qualities of the mind," in S3b means essentially the same thing as the little word "wit" in S3c, and "beauty" in S3c is the simple equivalent of "the composition of the man" in S3b. In column 2, "cause" and "move" are synonymous, and in column 6 "like" and "love" seem not to carry the different weight that they normally do in literary use. This is a kind of super coherence with a minimum of development. The whole sentence, in fact, seems to have been designed with far more attention to sound and structure than to developmental thought.

S3 EXERCISES

Again, we have done most of the analytical work for you, but here are some synthetic exercises:

1. Paraphrase the meaning of S3 in the fewest possible
   words. Compare your version with those of others.
   Then consider the best version that anyone has been
   able to produce—closest paraphrase, fewest words.
   What has been gained or lost in the paraphrase?

2. Keeping S3a as it is, and following exactly the verbal
   structure of the original sentence, change all the nouns
   and verbs so that the sentence discusses some entirely
   different topic, such as the weather, an athletic event,
   Tarzan and Jane, your school, some news item, insects.
   . . . Remember to keep everything exactly in place
   while substituting new nouns and verbs for the old
   ones.

3. Try to present the ideas of Bacon's sentences (S1 or S2
   or both) in a sentence structured as nearly like S3 as
   you can manage.

4. Try to express the ideas of S3 in the structure of S1
   or S2.

5. Consider the extent to which you have succeeded in
   dealing with questions 2, 3, or 4 and the problems
   which made success difficult or prevented it.

S4

   Now if nature should intermit her course and leave altogether, though it were but for a while, the observation of
   her own laws; if those principal and mother elements of
   the world, whereof all things in this lower world are
   made, should lose the qualities which now they have; if
   the frame of that heavenly arch erected over our heads
   should loosen and dissolve itself; if the celestial spheres

should forget their wonted motions, and by irregular volubility turn themselves any way as it might happen; if the prince of the lights of heaven, which now as a giant doth run his unwearied course, should, as it were through a languishing faintness, begin to stand and to rest himself; if the moon should wander from her beaten way, the times and seasons of the year blend themselves by disordered and confused mixture, the winds breathe out their last gasp, the clouds yield no rain, the earth be defeated of heavenly influence, the fruits of the earth pine away as children at the withered breasts of their mother no longer able to yield them relief;—what would become of man himself, whom these things now do all serve?

RICHARD HOOKER

This extraordinary sentence has the true periodic structure. It is a syntactic unit which suspends its completion until almost the last word. In this case the sentence completes itself at the word "man" and is then extended by a subordinate clause—"whom these things now do all serve" —which is really an extension of the word "man" itself, a reminder of man's relation to the things mentioned in the first part of the sentence. The basic structure of this complex sentence follows a very simple pattern: if this . . . then what—or, if this should . . . then what would. . . . Once we are aware of this basic pattern we can see how extraordinarily unbalanced the sentence is. There are eleven distinct sections in the "if" part of the sentence, compared with a single unit in the "then what" part. The whole sentence is too large to be displayed on a single page, but we can get a sense of its structure by reproducing its main parts and indicating the things we have left out by ellipsis dots:

	1	2	3	4
S4a	if	nature	should	intermit and leave . . . ;
S4b	if	those . . . elements . . .	should	lose . . . ;
S4c	if	the frame of that . . . arch . . .	should	loosen and dissolve itself;
S4d	if	the celestial spheres	should	forget and turn . . . ;
S4e	if	the prince of the lights . . .	should	begin to stand and to rest himself;
S4f	if	the moon	should . . .	wander . . . ,
S4g		the times and seasons		blend themselves . . . ,
S4h		the winds		breathe out their last gasp,
S4i		the clouds		yield no rain,
S4j		the earth		be defeated . . . ,
S4k		the fruits of the earth		pine away . . . ;—

what would become of man . . . ?

S4 EXERCISES

ANALYTIC

1. Referring to the above display, consider the following questions:

    a. After S4f, columns 1 and 3 are blank. How do you account for this?

    b. The end-punctuation in column 4 changes after S4e. How do you account for this?

    c. After S4e, no words intervene between the subject in column 2 and the verb in column 3 or 4. How do you account for this?

    d. What do your answers to a, b, and c suggest about the developmental process in this sentence?

    e. Consider the items in column 2. In what ways do they make a coherent list? In what ways is the list developmental? Is the list progressively developmental or randomly developmental?

    f. Consider the items in column 4. In what ways do they make a coherent list? In what ways is the list developmental?

    g. Consider the items we have had to leave out of our structural display of the sentence. What function does each of them perform in its clause? in the whole sentence?

    h. Can you summarize the argument of the sentence briefly? How does the structure of the sentence contribute to the argument? How do the items you considered in question g contribute?

    i. What would you consider an appropriate word or phrase to describe the tone of the sentence? To what extent is the tone a matter of structure? a matter of the connotations of particular words, phrases, and images? (In trying to define exactly what *tone* is, you might start by thinking of it as the tone of voice that seems to animate the sentence—the way it ought to sound if interpreted orally.)

j. Can you find a rationale for the imbalance of the sentence—eleven units in the first part and one in the second?

SYNTHETIC

1. Preserving as much as possible of the structure of S4, use it to make an argument about some serious issue of the present day: political, environmental, social.

2. Preserving as much as possible of S4, use it to express an attitude on some trivial or inconsequential situation. What happens when you do this?

3. Take the sentence you have generated in response to question 1 and try to present the same argument through an entirely different structural pattern. Use as many sentences as you wish, but keep the whole sequence to the same length as S4. What are the strengths and weaknesses of both versions? How have you achieved coherence and development in the new structure you have made?

S5

She was puritan, like her father, high-minded, and really stern. Therefore the dusky, golden softness of this man's sensuous flame of life, that flowed off his flesh like the flame from a candle, not baffled and gripped into incandescence by thought and spirit as her life was, seemed to her something wonderful, beyond her.   D. H. LAWRENCE

These two sentences make a small sequence. They are connected in a casual relationship indicated by the word "Therefore." Later on we will look at the other interconnections between the two sentences, but first let us examine the structure of each sentence separately. The first consists of a simple, three-word unit, followed by parallel substitutions for the third word. In a structural display, the sentence will look something like this:

	1	2	3
S5a	She	was	puritan,
S5b			like her father,
S5c			high-minded,
and			
S5d			really stern.

This is the loosest kind of parallel construction. Column 3 is just a series of qualities, which could be longer or shorter because it is not tied to any other parallel series in the sentence. (Compare S1, for instance, with its two parallel columns.) The other two columns show ellipses after the first unit. The sentence is not periodic. It could end after the third word and we would feel no sense of syntactic incompleteness. The qualities in column 3 seem to have no necessary order. They could be rearranged without changing the sense or tone of the sentence much. The one item in column 3 that is least like the others grammatically is the phrase "like her father." If this phrase had been placed elsewhere—say, in S5a—it might seem less arbitrary in its location. Where it is, it seems casual, and the words after it come almost as afterthoughts, conversationally. This sentence is deliberately loose and conversational in its structure. The sentence that follows it is quite different. If we abstract from the second sentence its grammatical center or main syntactic unit, we get something like this: ". . . the softness . . . seemed . . . wonderful. . . ." There we have a grammatical subject in "softness" and its predication in "seemed . . . wonderful." In looking at the whole sentence, we should notice the distance between this subject and predicate. This sentence *is* periodic, holding its meaning suspended for completion until nearly the last word: "wonderful." We can also see that the grammatical subject does not really function by itself as the semantic or meaningful subject of the sentence. A special kind of softness—"the dusky, golden softness of this man's sensuous flame of life"—is the semantic subject of the sentence. And once that subject has been entirely expressed, the sentence could complete itself with the predication we have already abstracted: "The dusky golden softness of this man's sensuous flame of life . . . seemed to her wonderful." But what of the words that occupy the central part of the sentence, between this subject and predicate? This central part of the sentence amounts to a further elaboration of the subject in the form of a parenthetical addition to the sentence, embedded between subject and verb. This parenthetical element is what causes the suspense in the sentence and makes it periodic. If we look closely at it, we can see that the parenthetical interruption consists of two parts, divided by commas, which have certain elements of parallel construction that can be seen if we present the two parts in a structural display:

S5e   that flowed off his flesh like the flame from a candle
S5f   not baffled and gripped into incandescence by thought and spirit

These two units form an antithesis, with S5f working in contrast to S5e. The nature of this opposition between

S5e and S5f can be further clarified if we abstract from
each unit certain parallel but opposed items and rearrange
them so as to emphasize their opposition. Keeping to the
order of S5e, we can abstract three important lexical items:

flowed   flesh   flame (candle)

Now rearranging the items from S5f so as to show their
connections with the items in S5e, we can establish the
following pattern:

	1	2	3
S5e	flowed	flesh	flame—(candle)
S5f	baffled and gripped	thought and spirit	incandescence—(electric light)

Now each column contains coherent items: column 1, verbs
related to physical motion; column 2, nouns that name
human attributes; column 3, nouns that describe kinds of
lighting. Each column also shows a developmental contrast
between the items of S5e and S5f. "Flowed" signifies free
and easy motion; "baffled and gripped" as a unit signify
motion frustrated and retarded. "Flame from a candle"
signifies a soft, "natural" kind of light; "incandescence"
signifies a harsh "mechanical" kind of light.

When we look across the lines we can also notice some
interesting things. The sequence "flowed . . . flesh . . .
flame" is marked by a striking alliterative pattern of
sounds, while in S5b there is no similarity of sound at all
between word and word. The doubled verbs and nouns in
S5f (baffled-gripped and thought-spirit) contrast markedly
with the single words of S5e, and the four syllables of "incandescence" make the same kind of contrast with the
mono-syllabic simplicity of "flame." Once we are alerted

by the alliteration of S5e to look for further poetical effects, we can find them. "That flowed off his flesh like the flame from a candle" has a pronounced anapestic rhythm (da-dum-da-da-dum-da-da-dum-da-da-dum-da) which emphasizes the harmonious quality of the man's natural flame—an effect to which the alliteration also contributes. The unit "not baffled and gripped into incandescence by thought and spirit" has no such poetical effects. It is just serious, rather labored prose.

Lawrence has developed an elaborate metaphor in this sentence, through which he is contrasting the man's life style with the woman's. The man's life is like the candle flame, the woman's like an incandescent electric light—in which light is produced precisely by baffling and gripping the flow of electrons through a filament. And all of Lawrence's poetical effects are designed to reinforce this metaphorical contrast. Words like "baffled" and "gripped" carry their double load of meaning perfectly. They describe the physical process of incandescence and they relate to the mental qualities of thought and spirit which are responsible for the baffling and gripping. These qualities in turn are related to the puritanical high-mindedness and sternness that are presented in the previous sentence. They are an important force in the coherence of the whole sequence.

The ability to find or create such metaphors can hardly be taught formally. But we can try to learn from writers like Lawrence how to be aware of metaphor and other poetic effects, and how to use the structural resources of the English sentence so as to make the most of the metaphors we are fortunate enough to find. Metaphor, as we observed in the theoretical part of this book, is not simply a poetic effect; it is a fundamental quality of language. We are always using metaphors, with more or less awareness, more or less appropriateness.

S5   EXERCISES

ANALYTIC

We have done most of the analytic work on this sequence. But one question about our method should be raised at this point, and that is the question of how we arrived at the procedure we used. It would be nice (maybe) if there were a neat formula that could be applied to every problem in the analysis of prose. But there is not. Our method in this instance as in every other was largely dictated by the sequence we are examining. In approaching a sentence or sequence we must look for elements of coherence and development. We must try to recognize its important structural qualities and its other dominant features (like the elaborate metaphor in this instance) and find some way to display them that will reveal their functioning. This means that we must begin to recognize their features before we can find the best way of displaying them. Experience helps here, but there is always a certain amount of trial and error in this sort of procedure. You may be sure that the analysis you have just read is not the first we attempted on this sentence. It is, of course, the last—the best we could do. The one fundamental procedure we can suggest for beginning any analysis is to look for the grammatical basis of the sentence: locate the principal subject and the main verb; try to abstract from the sentence its basic pattern of predication. Then look for other features and try to find ways of displaying them for analysis.

SYNTHETIC

Since S5 is so dependent on metaphor, try to construct variations on it by modifying the metaphor. What can you do, for instance, with fluorescent lighting (as opposed to incandescent) or with lazer beams? Can you treat the qualities of a candle so as to generate a different effect from

Lawrence's? Try rewriting the sequence, preserving Lawrence's basic structure, and using some metaphors of light,
but altering these metaphors so as to change the tone and
meaning of the sequence. You might choose to focus your
beams on Tarzan and Jane, for instance, or some other
couple. But set for yourself the problem of describing two
contrasting life styles in terms of the metaphoric contrasts
you establish.

S6

> For some months now I have lived with my own youth
> and childhood, not always writing indeed but thinking of
> it almost every day, and I am sorrowful and disturbed. It
> is not that I have accomplished too few of my plans, for
> I am not ambitious; but when I think of all the books I
> have read, and of the wise words I have heard spoken,
> and the anxiety I have given to parents and grandparents,
> and of the hopes I have had, all life weighed in the scales
> of my own life seems to me a preparation for something
> that never happens.   W. B. YEATS

S6   EXERCISES

ANALYTIC

1.   Here we have two sentences. Describe the relationship
     between them. What makes the second sentence co-
     herent with the first one? In what ways does the second
     sentence develop out of and add to the first one?

2.   What is the relationship between the final clause of
     the first sentence and the opening clause? How does
     the conjunction "and" function here to introduce the
     last clause of the first sentence? Does it mean some-
     thing like "however"? "nevertheless"? "therefore"?

what? Why do you suppose Yeats chose "and" over some more narrowly limited conjunction?

3. What is the structure of the second sentence? Can you isolate the main subject and predicates? Why is there a semicolon after "ambitious"?

4. Make a structural display of the sentence beginning after the semi-colon. How does parallel construction operate in the sentence? What is its function?

SYNTHETIC

1. Change the last words of the first sentence to "joyful and soothed." Then, keeping as much of the structure of the second sentence as you can, make appropriate substitutions for such words as must be eliminated in order to adjust the second sentence to the revised meaning of the first.

2. Compare several responses to synthetic question 1 to see how different people went about the work of revising. Try to determine which revision is best—and why. Consider the reasons why different people made different choices about which words to change and what substitutes to employ.

S7

No place affords a more striking conviction of the vanity of human hopes, than a public library; for who can see the wall crowded on every side by mighty volumes, the works of laborious meditation, and accurate inquiry, now scarcely known but by the catalogue, and preserved only to increase the pomp of learning, without considering how many hours have been wasted in vain endeavour, how often imagination has anticipated the praises of futurity,

how many statues have been raised to the eye of vanity,
how many ideal converts have elevated zeal, how often
wit has exulted in the eternal infamy of his antagonists,
and dogmatism has delighted in the gradual advances of
his authority, the immutability of his degrees, and the
perpetuity of his power?   SAMUEL JOHNSON

S7 EXERCISES

ANALYTIC

1. Compare the relationship between the parts of this
   sentence before and after the semi-colon with that
   between the two sentences in S6. In what ways are the
   relationships between the parts in these two sequences
   similar? How do they differ?

2. In what ways are the ideas and attitudes of S6 and S7
   similar? How do they differ?

3. Consider Johnson's vocabulary. How would you describe his choice of words? How would you compare
   his diction to that of the other writers whose work
   appears in this section of the book?

4. The aspect of metaphorical language that Johnson uses
   most is personification. Locate as many instances of
   personification in the sequence as you can, and discuss
   their function or functions.

5. Isolate the basic elements of Johnson's sentence. Then
   make a structural display of its construction. How does
   Johnson's use of parallelism compare to Yeats's in S6?
   How many levels of parallel structure do you find in
   Johnson's sentence? Why does he use two ways of
   introducing his major parallel elements ("how many"
   and "how often") and how does he use these two
   ways?

6. How carefully are the elements in Johnson's parallel constructions balanced against one another? When you read the vertical columns in your structural display, what patterns emerge?

SYNTHETIC

1. Compile a list of alternatives for the last word in the first clause of this sentence—instead of "library" think of "theater," "rest room," etc. Then try substituting one of these alternative words for "library" and revising the sentence accordingly. Once again, try to keep as much of Johnson's structure as you can, and preserve as many of his words as you can. The new elements you introduce should, of course, fit in with the Johnsonian elements you have preserved.

2. Rewrite the whole of S7 in a totally different style, but preserving as many of its ideas as you can. You might, for instance, try to avoid all long words, or try to achieve a written style based on current slang—but try to find an equivalent for each of Johnson's phrases in whatever style you adopt, and try to keep this style as consistent as possible.

S8

The church is Catholic, universal, so are all her actions; all that she does belongs to all. When she baptizes a child, that action concerns me; for that child is thereby connected to that body which is my head too, and ingrafted into that body whereof I am a member. And when she buries a man, that action concerns me: all mankind is of one author, and is one volume; when one man dies, one chapter is not torn out of the book, but translated; God employs several translators; some pieces are translated by age, some by sickness, some by war, some by justice; but God's hand is in every translation, and his hand shall bind up all our scattered leaves again for that library where every book shall lie open to one another.   JOHN DONNE

S8 EXERCISES

ANALYTIC

1. This sequence begins with a general statement that is then illustrated with respect to baptism and death. The universality of death is then developed in an extended metaphor throughout the last sentence. Begin by circling all the words in the sentence which contribute to that metaphor. Be sure you have them all. Then list them in a single column in order of their appearance.

2. Using the list you have compiled, discuss the operation of Donne's extended metaphor. Consider its contribution to the coherence and development of the whole sequence. How many aspects of the metaphor can you distinguish? Does it operate mainly through nouns? verbs? adjectives? What dictates the arrangement of the different aspects of metaphor? Is the sentence random or progressive in its development?

3. The metaphor in the last sentence is supported by some parallel construction. Make a structural display of the sentence. Compare the use of parallelism here with its use in S7.

4. This sequence and S7 share some images. Can you describe analytically the different way these images function in the two sequences?

5. Compare the use of metaphorical language in this sequence and S7; in this sequence and S5; in this sentence and S4.

Synthetic

1. Rewrite S8, keeping as many of its ideas as possible, but scrupulously avoiding all use of metaphor. This will not be easy, but do the best you can. Try to work very deliberately, so that when you are finished you can discuss the ideas in the sequence for which you had the most difficulty in finding non-metaphorical equivalents.

2. Rewrite the last sentence of S8, substituting another extended metaphor for the one Donne has used. Try to make the same points, but in terms of your new metaphor. Let your sentence become ridiculous, if that is the direction it takes, but keep the metaphor intelligible and consistent throughout the sentence. Compare your results with others'. What makes for success in this sort of exercise?

S9

> If you could make the yellow flames of candles in the sun; that shines on steel of bayonets freshly oiled and yellow patent leather belts of those who guard the Host; or hunt in pairs through scrub oak in the mountains for the ones who fell into the trap at Deva (it was a bad long way to come from the Café Rotonde to be garotted in a drafty room with consolation of the church at order of the state, acquitted once and held until the captain general of Burgos reversed the finding of the court) and in the same town where Loyola got his wound that made him think, the bravest of those who were betrayed that year dove from the balcony onto the paving of the court, head first, because he had sworn they would not kill him; (his mother tried to make him promise not to take his life because she worried most about his soul but he dove well

and cleanly with his hands tied while they walked with him praying); if I could make him; make a bishop; make Candido Tiebas and Toron; make clouds come fast in shadows moving over wheat and the small, careful stepping horses; the smell of olive oil; the feel of leather; rope soled shoes; the loops of twisted garlics; earthen pots; saddle bags carried across the shoulder; wine skins; the pitchforks made of natural wood (the tines were branches); the early morning smells; the cold mountain nights and long hot days of summer, with always trees and shade under the trees, then you would have a little of Navarra.

ERNEST HEMINGWAY

S9   EXERCISES

ANALYTIC

1.   Make a structural display of this sentence.

2.   Which of the earlier sentences or sequences does it most resemble in structure? Discuss the resemblance. If you find that S9 resembles more than one of the previous sentences in structure, discuss the others, too.

3.   The materials in this sentence could have been broken into many short sentences. Hemingway knows how to write short sentences. He writes them cleanly and well. So why do you suppose he chose to use a long sentence in this case? In other words, what effects do you feel he is aiming at in this sentence?

4.   In its original context this sentence is followed by another. Together, the two sentences stand as a separate paragraph. The sentence which completes the paragraph is this: "But it's not in this book." Discuss the two sentences as a sequence. What do they accomplish together? How?

5. Consider the question of tone in this sentence. How would you describe the tone? How is it achieved?

6. Using your structural display, discuss the rhythm of this sentence and the development of its elements. Is it random or progressive? Does it move at a steady pace or vary its rhythm? Does it stay on one level or move to a climax?

7. What would happen to the sentence if the last clause were made the first, with the rest of the sentence following?

8. Look up Navarra in an encyclopedia or a geography book. (It is in northern Spain.) Compare Hemingway's description to the others you find. What are the virtues and limitations of each?

SYNTHETIC

1. Following Hemingway's structure as closely as possible, write a sentence about a place that you know and love. Try to make the same sorts of appeals to our physical senses and our sense of history that he makes, but be as accurate and faithful to the place as you can be. Before you start, you might want to make sure you understand the Hemingway thoroughly. What, for instance, is that business about Loyola and the wound that made him think? The general frame of reference has to do with actions of the Spanish Civil War of the 1930's, but Loyola adds another context.

2. Again following Hemingway's structure, write about a place that you detest. Does this structure work equally well for both emotions?

S10

It was a town of red brick, or of brick that would have been red if the smoke and ashes would have allowed it; but as matters stood it was a town of unnatural red and black like the painted face of a savage. It was a town of machinery and tall chimneys, out of which interminable serpents of smoke trailed themselves for ever and ever, and never got uncoiled. It had a black canal in it, and a river that ran purple with ill-smelling dye, and vast piles of building full of windows where there was a rattling and a trembling all day long, and where the piston of the steam engine worked monotonously up and down, like the head of an elephant in a state of melancholy madness. It contained several large streets all very like one another, and many small streets still more like one another, inhabited by people equally like one another, who all went in and out at the same hours, with the same sound upon the same pavements, to do the same work, and to whom every day was the same as yesterday and tomorrow, and every year the counterpart of the last and the next.

                                                        CHARLES DICKENS

S10   EXERCISES

ANALYTIC

1.   Make structural displays of the sentences in this sequence, to illustrate the way that the whole sequence depends on both parallel constructions and repetitions of whole words and phrases. Consider the function of this structure with respect to the intention of the passage. To what extent do the tone and meaning of the passage depend on the meanings of particular words and the effect of particular images? What does structure contribute to the total effect?

2. Compare this descriptive sequence with S9. How do
    you account for the difference in tone and attitude in
    the two passages? What role does sentence structure
    play in this? What about different kinds of words?
    Compare the use of pronouns, of nouns, of verbs, of
    adjectives in the two passages.

SYNTHETIC

1. Following Dickens's sentence structure as closely as
    possible, write a sentence about an ugly despicable
    place that you happen to know.

2. Now use Dickens's structure for a description of an
    engaging, attractive place.

3. Compare your responses to *these* synthetic questions
    with your responses to the synthetic questions on S9.
    What generalizations about the functions of structure
    and word choice can you make on the basis of your
    four descriptions? How does your experience compare
    with that of others who have done these exercises?

S11

   I'm perfectly aware that I'm in prison, that I'm a Negro,
   that I've been a rapist, and that I have a Higher Unedu-
   cation. I never know what significance I'm supposed to
   attach to these factors. But I have a suspicion that, because
   of these aspects of my character, "free-normal-educated"
   people rather expect me to be more reserved, penitent,
   remorseful, and not too quick to shoot off my mouth on
   certain subjects. But I let them down, disappoint them,
   make them gape at me in a sort of stupor, as if they're
   thinking: "You've got your nerve! Don't you realize that

you owe a debt to society?" My answer to all such thoughts lurking in their split-level heads, crouching behind their squinting bombardier eyes, is that the blood of Vietnamese peasants has paid off all my debts; that the Vietnamese people, afflicted with a rampant disease called Yankees, through their sufferings—as opposed to the "frustration" of fat-assed American geeks safe at home worrying over whether to have bacon, ham, or sausage with their grade-A eggs in the morning, while Vietnamese worry each morning whether the Yankees will gas them, burn them up, or blow away their humble pads in a hail of bombs—have cancelled all my IOUs. ELDRIDGE CLEAVER

S11   EXERCISES

1.   Make structural displays of the sentences in this sequence which use parallel constructions. What conclusions about Cleaver's use of parallelism can you reach on the basis of your displays?

2.   In the last sentence of this sequence, how does the parallism work to place certain ideas and images into relation with one another? (Read your columns vertically.)

3.   What is the basic sentence around which the entire last sentence is built? Why do you suppose Cleaver chose to expand that basic sentence in the way that he did?

4.   In what ways is the last sentence coherent with and developmental of the earlier part of the sequence? In what ways is it conclusive?

SYNTHETIC

1.   Try removing all the adjectives from this sequence and changing all the colloquial nouns and verbs to more

formal equivalents. What effect do these changes make in the passage?

2. Try keeping Cleaver's choice of words but breaking up his parallel constructions and eliminating the periodic suspense of the final sentence. How successfully can you rewrite the sequence without using any parallel constructions?

3. Using Cleaver's sequence as a structural model, imagine another sort of person, imprisoned in some other time at some other place, and express his attitude toward his situation. Make your vocabulary and grammar appropriate to the character you are creating. You may want to take a historical figure who has been imprisoned, or invent a man who might have been imprisoned in some actual historical situation that you know of. If you need to do some research, do it, but make your details as accurate as you can. Remember to follow Cleaver's structure.